John Knox for Armchair Theologians

Also Available in the Armchair Series

John Knox
for Armchair Theologians

SUZANNE MCDONALD

ILLUSTRATIONS BY RON HILL

WESTMINSTER
JOHN KNOX PRESS
LOUISVILLE · KENTUCKY

First edition
Published by Westminster John Knox Press
Louisville, Kentucky

13 14 15 16 17 18 19 20 21 22—10 9 8 7 6 5 4 3 2 1

Book design by Sharon Adams
Cover design by Jennifer K. Cox
Cover illustration: Ron Hill

Library of Congress Cataloging-in-Publication Data

McDonald, Suzanne
  John Knox for armchair theologians / Suzanne McDonald ;
illustrations by Ron Hill. — 1st ed.
     p. cm.
  Includes bibliographical references (p.   ) and index.
  ISBN 978-0-664-23669-4 (alk. paper)
  1. Knox, John, ca. 1514-1572. I. Title.
  BX9223.M335 2013
  230'.52092—dc23

                                           2012033624

Contents

Contents

Acknowledgments

This project has been tremendous fun! So my first "thank-you" has to go to Don McKim, who asked me to write it and with whom it is a joy to work. Many, many thanks to Ron Hill as well for bringing the text to life in his inimitable way.

It is a blessing to be at a liberal arts college that is so supportive of faculty who write as well as teach. I am deeply grateful to Calvin College for the periods of research leave that have made this book possible.

Needless to say, I am the only one to blame for any errors and infelicities here, but I am thankful for my colleagues Susan Felch and Karin Maag, whose careful reading has saved me from quite a few.

Thank you also to David Deters, friend and pastor extraordinaire, for your encouragement in so many ways. While I know you still don't particularly like Knox, I'm glad that reading this has meant that you don't dislike him quite as much as you did!

Finally, special thanks go to my parents, Bob and Annette. Your boundless enthusiasm for this book helped to keep me going when I was in danger of flagging, and your splendid ideas have done so much to improve it. I dedicate this to you with my love.

(RE)INTRODUCING JOHN KNOX

There are very few theologians whose lives have been quite as turbulent and dramatic as that of John Knox. His life could be the stuff of historical novels, from being a prisoner in chains on a French warship to being the fearless scourge of monarchs. The sixteenth-century equivalent of the gossip columns even managed to find plenty of material in his somewhat unorthodox domestic life for some scandalous rumormongering.

There are also very few theologians who could be named as a driving force in the shaping of a nation. You can't trace the history of the Scottish Reformation—a defining moment in Scotland's story—without placing the towering figure of Knox close to the center, theologically and politically. And a very ambivalent figure he is.

What is your picture of Knox, if you have one? A fiery preacher, fulminating from the pulpit? A haranguing bully who made Mary, Queen of Scots, cry? The writer of a book with the unforgettable title, *The First Blast of the Trumpet against the Monstrous Regiment of Women*? Or the patient, caring pastor whose letters were treasured for a lifetime? Or one-half of a popular husband and wife team whose supper invitations guaranteed a lively evening?

Knox is all of these things and more. If you have never encountered John Knox before, I hope this book will give you a rounded introduction to his life and writing. If you have already met Knox through cameo portraits or folklore, I would like to reintroduce him to you so that perhaps you will find that there is more to him than you thought. For everyone, I also hope that this book will help you to understand those aspects of Knox that you find difficult to like or relate to—even if you still find them difficult to like or relate to when you've finished!

If you have read other books in this Armchair series, this venture into the life and writings of John Knox is going to take a slightly different format to the usual. You might have seen in the table of contents that there are six chapters, and interspersed between the chapters some "Key Texts" sections. The chapters tell you the story of Knox's life. They will mention some of the works that he wrote and some of the theological ideas and issues but won't go into much detail about them. That is the task of the key texts sections. Each of these is designed to give you some more information on one or two significant works, either by Knox or strongly associated with Knox, in the period of his life covered by the preceding chapter. Especially if you are not very familiar with Knox's life and times, you might like to read the chapters straight through first, without pausing to turn to the key texts so that you can get an uninterrupted overview of his life. Then you can come back to the key texts for more about his writing and ideas, situated in the context of his life. Obviously, we can't cover everything that Knox wrote, or even very much detail on the texts that I've chosen to include. The task here is simply to shine a spotlight on some significant works and to highlight some themes that Knox draws out and develops over the course of his life. There are some suggestions for further reading at the end if you would like to find out more.

The reason for this approach is because while it's never possible to separate a theologian's ideas from his or her personal life story and historical context, for someone like Knox you can't even begin to understand his writings unless you also immerse yourself in his life and circumstances. In fact, it is only because he is in the thick of history-making events that he writes at all. Most of his writing is a direct response to presenting issues, and most of his theological thinking is worked out in the midst of dramatic circumstances as they unfold. You will soon see—when you plunge into his life story—that Knox is not a man with much leisure time to sit down and write on matters that don't have an immediate bearing on the issues swirling around him. And in any case, he is not the kind of person to produce extended works of theology. He sees his calling to be above all a prophet, a preacher, and a pastor, not a theologian and writer. In his own words, he says, "For considering myself rather called of God to instruct the ignorant, comfort the sorrowful, confirm the weak and rebuke the proud by tongue and lively voice in these most corrupt days, than to compose books for the age to come. . . . I decreed to contain myself within the bonds of that vocation whereunto I found myself especially called."[1]

This means that we cannot expect to be able to construct neat accounts of "Knox's theology of *x*." He writes only one large treatise on a particular theological topic (predestination). For most issues we have to do what Knox himself did: explore his thought in the context of his responses to whatever crises were confronting him at the time. The best way to get a sense of his theological thinking and its development is to follow along with Knox as he writes rather than trying to tell his life story and then stand back and reflect on what he wrote in abstraction from what was happening in his life when he wrote it. His theological ideas are woven into the story of his life because that is how his theological ideas were developed and expressed. This is why what you have here is an account of his work that is interspersed, like pauses for breath, in the fast-paced story of his life.

Although it is always arbitrary to divide someone's life up into neat periods, Knox's story does allow us to do this in a more straightforward way than others' stories. The first chapter will take us from Knox's birth in 1514 until the end of his time as a galley slave in 1549. The key text that goes with this part of his life is his revision of a treatise on the central Protestant doctrine of justification by faith.

The next phase of his life sees him in England during the reign of the Protestant King Edward VI, until his exile in 1554, when Edward's Roman Catholic half-sister, Mary Tudor, ascends the throne. The key texts associated with this chapter are a tract against the Roman Catholic understanding of the Mass and some public letters that he wrote to Protestants in England with advice on how to live under the new Roman Catholic regime.

For Knox, exile was both invigorating and turbulent. He spent time in Geneva and in Frankfurt where he was up to

his neck in the troubles of the church for English exiles. He met and corresponded with some of the most important theologians of his day, including John Calvin. He wrote his most famous book. He kept a close eye on the situation in his homeland of Scotland and traveled there to assist the cause of Protestantism. The key texts related to this period are his book, *The First Blast of the Trumpet against the Monstrous Regiment of Women,* and his public letters to Scotland, urging resistance to the Roman Catholic ruler, the regent Mary of Guise.

In 1559, Knox left exile to return to his native country and to a Protestant revolution that his letters had helped to provoke and his presence helped to inspire. Chapter 4 charts Scotland's steps toward becoming an officially Protestant country and Knox's role in that. The key texts here are the founding documents of that Protestant settlement:

the *Book of Common Order*, the *Book of Discipline*, and *The Scots Confession*. Although Knox is not the sole author of any of these, he is involved in writing all of them, and they show us the priorities of the movement that Knox had done so much to shape. A look at *The Scots Confession* also means a brief consideration of Knox's own writings on predestination and the Lord's Supper.

Chapter 5 opens with Knox thundering from the pulpit at St. Giles in Edinburgh with even more vigor than before as Mary, Queen of Scots, arrives in 1561 to take personal control of her realm and then flounders as her life and reign descend into chaos. With Knox increasingly on the margins when it comes to official political and theological life and declining in health, the chapter closes with Knox barely able to whisper his sermons and with his death in 1572. The final key text is his five-volume work *The History of the Reformation in Scotland*.

The last chapter is devoted to the other women in Knox's life. Most of us who know a little bit about Knox from what we have learned in school, in history books, on the Internet, or from folklore, know about Knox and a lot of rulers called Mary: Mary Tudor of England; Mary of Guise, the Regent of Scotland; and the regent's daughter Mary, Queen of Scots. How many know about Knox and Elizabeth Bowes? Or Anne Lock? Or his two wives, Marjorie and Margaret?

Painting a fuller portrait of Knox also means helping to erase caricatures of him. This is nowhere more clearly illustrated than in the popular perception of Knox and women. The persistent myth is simple: Knox hated women and did not know how to cope with them or treat them with the respect due to any fellow human being. If all we know about him is that he wrote a book against women rulers and that he berated poor Mary Queen of Scots so much that he reduced her to tears (tears more of frustration and fury,

incidentally, than intimidation), then perhaps the stereotype is no surprise. The closing chapter of this book reflects on how Knox engages with the less-famous but equally important women in his life. I hope it will help us to see that the caricature of Knox as nothing more than a misogynist oaf is unwarranted.

Following from this, the conclusion helps us to ask some questions about Knox for today. Where do we continue to see the legacy of this sixteenth-century firebrand prophet and preacher, and what can he still teach us?

CHAPTER ONE

From Roman Catholic Priest to Protestant Galley Slave

We know almost nothing about John Knox's early life. We can't even be sure of exactly when he was born, although most historians are now convinced that he was born in 1514.[1] We do know that he was born in the town of Haddington in Scotland, which is about twenty miles east of Edinburgh.

His father, William, was probably either a merchant or a craftsman, but again we can't be sure. We don't know his mother's first name, but her maiden name was Sinclair, and as Knox was beginning to make his way in the world, after his time at university, his mother's relations were on hand to help him. As for his very early years, it seems as though both his parents died when he was young, so it is likely that relatives looked after him and his older brother, William. We can assume that he attended a local school, and we know that he went to the University of St Andrews (given his age, probably in about 1529), although we can't even be sure that he graduated because his name doesn't appear in the records. This is almost certainly a problem with the record keeping, though, rather than any failings on Knox's part! With his brother William setting up his career as a merchant, John was intended for the priesthood, and that is the path he followed. As was customary, he first took an arts degree and then embarked on his theological studies. He is likely to have studied under the renowned Scottish scholastic theologian John Mair (sometimes spelled "Major"), who had previously taught at the highly prestigious Sorbonne University in Paris and who taught at the University of St Andrews in the early1530s.

St Andrews must have been abuzz with the controversy raised by Protestant ideas while Knox was a student. After all, Patrick Hamilton had been burned at the stake for heresy there in 1528. Hamilton had encountered Lutheran ideas while studying in Europe and had returned to Scotland full of zeal for the new movement. Even so, there are absolutely no signs that Knox had any Protestant convictions at this period in his life. In fact, he seems to have sought a dispensation to be ordained to the Roman Catholic priesthood somewhat earlier than usual. He became a priest shortly after being ordained a deacon in 1536, at the age of 22. He had no luck finding a parish though, and by 1540 we find him working as a notary apostolic (a minor legal position in the church court system) close to his hometown of Haddington. It looks as though he probably lived with some of his mother's relatives for a time and was involved in assisting them with legal matters. He also earned some additional money tutoring the sons of some of the local gentry.

This brings us to the early 1540s and to the verge of a major transition in Knox's life. Before exploring that, we need to pause and fill in some historical details so that we can place Knox in the context of the situation in Scotland, and also of the wider Reformation movement in Europe. From this point onward much of Knox's life and writing will be bound up with momentous historical events, and without some background and an ongoing description of the major political events swirling around him, Knox's life and his theological work will make no sense. Obviously, it is impossible to truly understand any theologian apart from an awareness of his or her personal and historical context, but political and theological controversy will combine with particular intensity for Knox over the next thirty years. Knox

himself will choose to chronicle that history, and his own role in it, in his *History of the Reformation in Scotland*.[2]

We will start with a wide lens—a snapshot of aspects of the situation in continental Europe—and then we'll narrow the focus to England and Scotland as Knox, quietly getting on with being a lawyer and tutor, is about to take steps that will set the course for the remainder of his life.[3]

Europe's House Divided

So, what was the situation by the early 1540s? Well, the Protestant Reformation had been under way in Europe for over twenty years. Martin Luther will die in 1546, just as war is about to break out between the German principalities that have adopted his reforming principles and the forces of the Roman Catholic Emperor Charles V. Ulrich Zwingli, spearhead of the Protestant movement in Zurich in the 1520s, died in battle a decade earlier in 1531. The city-state of Geneva became Protestant in 1536, with John Calvin briefly assisting the initial leaders of the Reformation there until he and they were all exiled in 1538. In 1541, the City Council of Geneva begged and pleaded for Calvin to return. He did, and would remain there for the rest of his life, seeking to transform the city into a beacon of Reformed Protestantism and a powerhouse of Reformed mission to his native France.

What of the Roman Catholics? A concerted official response from the Papacy to the Protestant Reformation was slow in coming, but the Society of Jesus (the Jesuits), which was founded by Ignatius of Loyola and would become central to the Counter-Reformation movement, received official confirmation as a Roman Catholic order in 1540. Five years later, Pope Pius III summoned the Council of Trent, which continued to meet off and on for the next two decades, with the final session taking place in 1563. The council set in place not only the official Roman Catholic doctrinal response to the challenges of the Protestant Reformation but also the internal reforms needed to combat some of the most flagrant abuses and inadequacies that the Protestant Reformation had exploited to gain support.

It is within this context of "Europe's house divided," to borrow the subtitle of a very fine study of the period, that we now also need to give a sketch of the situation in England and Scotland because it won't be long before Knox will be striding across the stage of both countries. Henry VIII of England was declared the Supreme Head of the English Church by an Act of Parliament in 1534, the culmination of

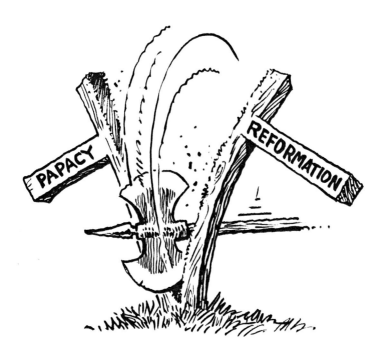

a process of breaking away from Rome that had been under way for several years, due to the Pope's refusal to grant Henry a divorce. Henry was much clearer (and happier) about the political and financial implications of severing ties with the Pope than he was about replacing Roman Catholic doctrines and practices with Protestant ones, as many were to discover to their cost. He did flirt with some Protestant ideas—at one stage he required all parish churches to acquire an English Bible, for example. By and large, before the Reformation, Bibles were in Latin and few people had access to them. One of the main desires of the Protestant Reformation was to give as many people as possible access to the Bible in their own languages. So it seemed as though Henry was encouraging Protestant ideas, at least for a while. But then in 1539 he also imposed the death penalty for the denial of transubstantiation. Transubstantiation is the understanding that while the outward appearance (or "accidents") of the bread and the wine at the sacrament of the Mass remains the same, when the priest says the words of consecration over them their inner essence (or "substance") is changed into the body and the blood of Jesus. While the various branches of Protestantism had different understandings of what was and wasn't going on in the sacrament, they all denied transubstantiation, so Henry's imposition of the death penalty for denying it was intended to cover any and all shades of non-Roman Catholic opinion on the subject. He also did a backflip on giving people access to the Bible in English. In 1543, he decided to restrict access to the English Bible to the nobility. Continuing to let ordinary people have access to the Bible for themselves, he decided, was far too dangerous.

Meanwhile in Scotland, things were much simpler. King James V remained staunch in his allegiance to the Papacy in spite of Henry VIII's urgings to join him in breaking away from Rome. James cemented his adherence to Roman Catholicism by marrying a daughter of the King of France, and then after she died he married the widowed Mary of Guise, a member of one of the most powerful aristocratic families in France. Scotland's rulers had often looked to France as an ally against the English, and this will be a recurring theme throughout the turbulent years of Knox's life.

Henry VIII considered both of these marriages to be provocative, to say the least. A meeting was arranged between the two monarchs, to take place at York in 1541, in an endeavor to diffuse the simmering tensions. At the last moment, however, James decided not to bother turning up. Henry was furious. He launched an English invasion of Scotland, and in 1542 James V's army was defeated at Solway Moss. James died shortly afterward, leaving his six-day-old daughter Mary as Queen of Scotland. James Hamilton, Earl of Arran, was appointed regent to rule on her behalf, and part of the peace negotiations with Henry included the promise that Mary would marry Henry VIII's son, Edward. Presumably as an attempt to demonstrate his enthusiasm for the implications of such a match, Arran began to encourage the spread of Protestantism in Scotland, allowing Protestant preaching and the distribution of Bibles in English. This is more than a little ironic because as we've just seen it isn't long after this that Henry bans the English Bible in England for anyone other than the upper classes. But all of this did have some unintended consequences for the life of one John Knox.

Back to Knox

These hopeful signs that Protestantism might be allowed to take root in Scotland encouraged an important Protestant figure, George Wishart, to return to his native land. This is

when major historical events and the life of John Knox first collide in a significant way. Wishart fled Scotland after a charge of heresy in 1538, spending the following years in exile. He arrived in Scotland again in 1543 and began an action-packed preaching tour, including surviving an assassination attempt in Dundee. He eventually made his way to Edinburgh and then to Knox's hometown of Haddington, where he turned Knox's life upside down. Knox doesn't actually give us any details about his conversion to Protestantism, but we do know that he was already a Protestant by the time he heard Wishart. He says that before Wishart's arrival in the area he had already heard some

Protestant preachers and had given his qualified approval to them. It was George Wishart's preaching, though, and the witness of his life and death, that were to inspire Knox for the rest of his life. Knox became one of Wishart's close associates and, in effect, one of his bodyguards. Apparently, he would often be called on to hold the two-handed broadsword before Wishart to protect him when in public.

Meanwhile, the political temperature for Protestantism in Scotland had cooled rapidly. Mary of Guise, the widow of James V and mother of the infant Queen Mary, strongly opposed any idea of a marriage between her daughter and Prince Edward of England, as did Cardinal Beaton, the Archbishop of St Andrews and Chancellor of Scotland. Beaton persuaded Arran to break the marriage treaty with Henry VIII in favor of a much more traditional alliance between France and Scotland. The new fiancé in prospect for the infant Queen Mary was to be no less than the heir to the French throne. For good measure, Cardinal Beaton humiliated Regent Arran by forcing him to do public penance for having sought an alliance between little Catholic Mary and those nasty English heretics. Henry VIII was not amused, and once again, he launched a series of raids on southern Scotland, with his army reaching as far as Edinburgh.

In the midst of all this turmoil, and with the renewed ascendency of Roman Catholic interests in Scottish politics, Knox's hero, George Wishart, was betrayed. He was in Haddington in January 1546, having just preached what was to be his final sermon, and was about to go and stay at the home of a member of the local gentry. As always, Knox picked up the broadsword and prepared to set out with him. Wishart, apparently knowing what was to come, refused to allow Knox to accompany him, and under protest Knox returned to his home. That night, Wishart was arrested and eventually taken to Cardinal Beaton's castle in

St Andrews where he was tried and condemned for heresy and then burned at the stake outside the castle on March 1, 1546. At the end of May that year, a group of Protestant gentry took their revenge by gaining entry to the castle and assassinating the Cardinal. Having taken over the castle, they were besieged by government forces, but somewhat half-heartedly because the Earl of Arran's young son was in the castle too, which rather complicated matters. In fact, it had been the Cardinal who had taken Arran's son hostage, just to make sure that Arran didn't change his mind about the wisdom of a French marriage for Mary over an English one. Since the poor lad was still there when the Protestants murdered the Cardinal and took his castle, he proved a useful hostage for them to keep as well. As the siege dragged on, those inside the castle received some supplies by sea and were also able to get word out to Henry VIII, pleading with him to send help. A truce of sorts was made, allowing those inside the castle to come and go freely, and scores of people arrived to support them. Among them was John Knox, and with him went two of the boys he was tutoring, with the enthusiastic support of their parents. Knox continued to tutor the boys while in St Andrews, and as we will see, it is as a result of this that Knox preached his first Protestant sermon.

Called to Be a Protestant Prophet

Interestingly, while Knox gives us no hints in *The History of the Reformation in Scotland* as to exactly when or how he was converted to Protestantism, he gives us a good deal of information about the life-changing moment when he took up the mantle of what he felt to be his prophetic preaching vocation.[4] He was teaching the boys about the Gospel of John, giving them their lessons in the castle chapel. Word spread, and many came to listen. As a result of what they heard, Knox was privately urged to become a preacher, but he refused, unsure of whether this was a legitimate calling of God. Another Protestant preacher exhorted him from the pulpit not to deny his vocation, and there were shouts of support from the congregation. That prompted Knox to withdraw for several days of prayer and solitude. It is typical of Knox, though, that it was combat rather than attempts at persuasion that finally tipped the balance. Hearing a sermon in defense of Roman Catholicism at the parish church, Knox sprang up and challenged the preacher to a debate. In a battle of sermons, Knox preached for the very first time at the parish church the following Sunday. Public disputations followed, until it became clear to the authorities that Knox was rather too good at them. It was also decided that all the learned men of the university would be invited to preach on Sundays at the parish

11

church—a lengthy list that would keep Knox out of the pulpit for some time to come! That was hardly going to be enough to silence Knox. He went there to preach on weekdays instead.

Knox was convinced from the moment he accepted the genuineness of his call to preach that he had indeed been singled out by God to be an instrument for the reforming of God's church. Over and over again, throughout the rest of his life, he would hark back to this time when he reached the assurance that he had heard the call of God in the summons to preach, seeing this as legitimating his ministry and his role as a leader in the Reformation movement. Knox's self-understanding was strongly shaped by identification with the Old Testament prophets. Like them he considered himself to

have been summoned by God to be a mouthpiece to pro-
claim the present will of God at a period of crisis for God's
people, and to warn of God's punishment for the doubters
and the backsliders, and also to prophesy concerning the
future consequences of obedience and disobedience to God.

For the moment, though, Knox didn't have long to exercise his preaching ministry in St Andrews. In June 1547, the
truce between the government and the Protestants who had
seized the castle broke down. The Protestants, their numbers increased by those like Knox who had chosen to come
and join them, withdrew to the castle and the siege
resumed. Shortly afterward, those inside rejoiced to see
some ships arriving—until they realized that instead of the
hoped-for English help, the ships were French. The situation was hopeless, and the Protestants surrendered. They
were taken on board the French ships, under the impression
that they would be set free for a life in exile when they
reached shore. Instead, the gentry were taken to be held
captive at various locations in France. The rest, Knox
included, became galley slaves for the French fleet, chained
by the legs, six men to an oar. In a bitter irony, Knox ended
up as part of the fleet that sailed to the aid of Mary of Guise,
now Regent of Scotland, against the English. During this
time he became desperately ill. His ship was in the Tay Estuary, besieging Broughty Castle, and in an attempt to keep
him going, a friend urged him to try to look toward the
shore, hoping that the sight of his native land would inspire
him. He looked southward, toward Fife, and saw the spires
and towers of St Andrews. In *The History of the Reformation
in Scotland* he says that he remarked: "I see the steeple of
that place where God first in public opened my mouth to
his glory. . . . I am fully persuaded, how weak that ever I
now appear, that I shall not depart this life till that my
tongue shall glorify his godly name in that same place."[5]

The physical conditions (and the food) were grim for the galley slaves, and Knox's health was permanently damaged from the illnesses and hardships he suffered. Worst of all, as far as Knox was concerned, the galley slaves were forced to attend Mass and hear such things as the French crew singing the Salve Regina (a prayer to the Virgin Mary, imploring her intercession) every Saturday night. He says that the galley slaves pulled their caps over their ears in protest. At one point their captors also tried to force them to kiss a statuette of the Virgin Mary. Knox tells us that "a Scotsman" (almost certainly Knox himself) tossed it into the water with the words, "let Our Lady now save herself: she is light enough; let her learn to swim." Apparently their captors didn't try that again.[6]

This was Knox's life for almost two years, until in March 1549 he was released. He does not tell us why, and historians have never found out. It is possible that it involved some intervention by the English. In any case, England is where he ends up next.

Before we join him there, though, the first of our key texts makes clear that there really is no stopping determined theologians.

Key Texts 1

Balnaves's Treatise on Justification

You wouldn't have thought Knox would have had much time or energy left for reading and writing while he was a galley slave, would you? And you wouldn't have thought that it was an easy matter for someone who was imprisoned in a castle in Rouen to forward a theological treatise to Mr. John Knox, Scottish prisoner-of-war care of a French ship, somewhere. But thanks to mutual friends, this is what happened. It helped that the ship on which Knox found himself was moored at Rouen for a while. As all of this indicates, though, there really was no stopping Knox and his fellow Scottish Protestants in their passionate commitment to the gospel as they understood it.

Henry Balnaves was one of the leading Protestant figures in St Andrews Castle, and one of the men who most strongly urged Knox to become a preacher. From his prison cell, he wrote a treatise on the doctrine of justification—that is to say, how we are set right with God. This is one of *the* major dividing issues of the Reformation, and Balnaves was strongly influenced by Martin Luther's position on the subject: that we are justified by grace through faith alone. That is, we are set right with God only by faith and faith itself is a gift of God's grace, not something we can muster up by ourselves from within ourselves. This means that we are not set right with God by any works that we do, whether those are moral good deeds or participating in the sacraments of the church or doing things like going on pilgrimages. The only way that we are justified before God is by faith in Jesus Christ and what he has done to obtain the forgiveness of our sins. Jesus' own righteousness before the Father is imputed to us through our union with him by the Spirit through faith, in what theologians call the "wondrous exchange." Luther himself describes this in terms of a marriage union between Christ and the Christian, in which, in typically blunt terms, what is ours (sin, death, and damnation) becomes Christ's, and what is his (grace, life, and salvation) becomes ours.[7] It is not that what we do—our works—do not matter to God, but they do not contribute to setting us right with him. Rather, works that are pleasing to God are the fruits of our justification and will show the genuineness of our faith.

These are the kinds of views that Balnaves endorsed and expressed, and he wanted Knox's opinion of his work. It was high. Receiving it clearly rejoiced Knox's heart. It eased his aching muscles and soothed the blisters on his hands enough for him to enthusiastically restructure and edit Balnaves's treatise in the hopes of seeing it published and disseminated as quickly as possible in Scotland. In fact, Knox's

edited manuscript was lost in transit and was only published when it resurfaced in 1584, twelve years after Knox's death. Even so, this early example of Knox's theological writing gives us some important insights into key themes that will continue to shape his life as a Protestant preacher and prophet.

In addition to dividing Balnaves's manuscript into chapters, Knox sought to make it more accessible to a wider audience by providing a synopsis of the argument of each chapter, in effect creating a ten-page summary of the whole treatise. It is through this summary—which very much filters Balnaves through Knox's own emphases—that we learn a good deal about Knox's theological style and priorities.

Obviously, we learn of Knox's enthusiastic commitment to one of the central planks of Protestantism, the doctrine of justification by grace through faith. It has been rightly pointed out that Knox's summary can stand on its own as a '*tour de force* against what Luther called 'works righteousness.'"[8]

Some Recurring Themes

In this text we also see Knox's decided preference for drawing on the Old Testament to provide examples to illustrate his major theological points. Throughout his life, Knox will make constant parallels between the crises in England and Scotland and the situation of God's covenant people Israel in the Old Testament, most particularly in their impending and actual exile as this is set forth in the prophets Isaiah, Jeremiah, and Ezekiel. Those prophets will also be a model for his own understanding of his calling. Already, in his summary of Balnaves's treatise, it is noticeable that he places much greater emphasis on Old Testament analogies and illustrations than is the case in Balnaves's actual text.

In addition to this early indication that he finds considerable inspiration in the Old Testament we find another theme that will be close to Knox's heart throughout the exercise of his calling: a horror of idolatry. Knox understands idolatry not simply in terms of worshiping false gods,

but, much more importantly in the context of the Reformation battles, in terms of worshiping the one true God falsely. For Knox, this means above all adopting practices and ceremonies in worship that do not have explicit scriptural warrant. As we will see, throughout his life Knox took a far harder line than many of his fellow Protestants, including Calvin, on the question of what is to be permitted and forbidden in services, on issues ranging from what ministers should wear, to forms of prayer, to how people should receive communion. Above all, the chief form of idolatrous, false worship against which Knox railed from the moment he became a public prophet of Protestantism was the Roman Catholic Mass. Hostility to the Mass was a prominent feature of Knox's preaching and disputation in St Andrews, and here in his summary of Balnaves's treatise it becomes a prime example of what Knox considers to be an idolatrous worship practice that had also become a good work through which to achieve right standing with God. We will have more to say about Knox's views of the Mass in the next key texts section. Now, though, it is time to join Knox as a free man, as he is about to exert his influence on the English Reformation.

CHAPTER TWO

From England to Exile

When Knox reached England, he rapidly made his way to London where he received a warm welcome and was introduced at the court of Edward VI. It is possible that he preached before the court almost immediately, since there is a record of the Privy Council paying him £5 on April 7, 1549. After the death of Henry VIII in 1547, the situation in England had changed considerably. As we have seen, Henry's desire for Protestant reforms in doctrine and worship was considerably less than his interest in the political implications of the split with Rome, and its financial benefits too, particularly from the dissolution of the monasteries.

With the very young but emphatically Protestant Edward VI on the throne and those in favor of further reform dominating the Privy Council, there was a flurry of Protestant legislation—laws to remove all images from churches, for example, and to insist (once again!) that all churches acquire a copy of the Bible in English and also that services be conducted in English rather than Latin. With the latter end in view, the first edition of the vernacular service book, the *Book of Common Prayer*, was published in 1549. The problem was, however, that while the nation was nominally Protestant, many areas of the country (and the majority of the citizens) retained the practices and piety of the "old religion" of Roman Catholicism. Implementation of the laws and enthusiasm for Protestantism generally was decidedly patchy outside London and was not helped by a severe shortage of Protestant preachers. So Knox's arrival seemed like a literal godsend: a fiery preacher just waiting to be let loose.

A Blazing Torch for the Benighted North . . .

Knox was asked to go to Berwick-upon-Tweed. This town, on the border with his native Scotland, was considered to be one of the dark corners of England, noted not only for its stubborn Roman Catholicism but also for its immorality and violence. It appears that Knox had a considerable effect on the piety and morals of the town while he preached there. He certainly had a very dramatic effect on the inhabitants of nearby Norham Castle. Elizabeth Bowes, the wife of the Castle's governor, converted to Protestantism, as did one of her daughters, Marjorie. Knox delicately negotiated the intense friendship of Elizabeth—by letter and in person—over the following decades, and Marjorie was to become his first wife. Each of these women will therefore continue to make an appearance in the story of Knox's life, and we will have more to say about them and how they help us to understand Knox in the final chapter.

For the moment, though, it seems that Knox's preaching also had quite an effect on Cuthbert Tunstall, Bishop of Durham, who had voted against Edward VI's Protestant reforms and continued to maintain Roman Catholic doctrines and practices. He was troubled by Knox's inflammatory preaching, in particular his habit of speaking violently against the Mass (Tunstall would later write a treatise defending the Roman Catholic understanding of this). About a year after Knox arrived in Berwick, he was summoned to give an account of his preaching before the Council of the North, over which Tunstall presided. Knox launched into a vigorous attack on the Mass and a defense of the principle that only that which is mandated in Scripture is permissible in worship. At one point he refers to Nadab and Abihu, who offered incense before the Lord in ways contrary to the Lord's commands and were consumed by fire (Lev. 10:1–2). Here was a none-too-gentle reminder to his hearers of God's judgment against those who would dare to go beyond what is prescribed in his Word when it comes to worship practice.[1]

The next key texts section will explain some of the issues at stake in relation to this topic. In addition to his passionate theological objections to Roman Catholic beliefs about the Mass, hostility to it was a constant refrain in his preaching for another very important reason. The Mass was the nerve center of people's piety. He knew that to undermine the beliefs and practices associated with it would be to put an axe to the root of most people's adherence to Roman Catholicism.

To Kneel or Not to Kneel, That Is the Question!

No harm came to Knox from his appearance before the Council of the North, and neither did it have any moderating effect on his preaching. The following year Knox moved to Newcastle to continue his feisty preaching ministry there. When the Duke of Northumberland visited the city he summoned Knox to accompany him back to London where he was soon preaching before the King and court. This was the occasion for one of Knox's most notorious sermons. He was deeply frustrated by what he considered to be the slow pace and insufficient rigor of reform in the English church. Perhaps the most famous episode to highlight the gap between what Knox desired and what the English church was prepared to undertake is the case of the "Black Rubric." The year that Knox returned to London—1552—saw the appearance of a revised version of the *Book of Common Prayer*. While the 1552 version does indeed reflect the further reforms undertaken since the first edition of 1549, in Knox's view there were still too many lingering whiffs of Roman Catholic doctrines and practices. With the 1552 edition already at the printing press, Knox preached against it before the King and the court, and in particular against the fact that it advocated kneeling to receive communion. To Knox, this could not help but suggest the bodily presence of Christ in the elements, as maintained by the Roman Catholic doctrine of transubstantiation. He felt that this practice would continue to lead people to venerate the bread and the wine, which he considered to be at the heart of the idolatry of the Mass.

Such was his influence that following his sermon the printing of *The Book of Common Prayer* was suspended and an alteration was made. Kneeling was still required, but an

explanation was inserted—the "Black Rubric"—to clarify that the posture of kneeling was not in any way intended to signify adoration of the elements. This hardly satisfied Knox, of course, but it is a major demonstration of his power. All sorts of significant people who were pressing for further reform, such as John Hooper, Bishop of Gloucester, had already raised similar objections, but to no avail. After one sermon from Knox, the printing presses ground to a halt.

This whole episode and its outcome did leave Knox in a rather awkward spot, though. He had preached vigorously against the practice of kneeling to receive communion in his parishes in Northumberland and had instigated the practice of having his parishioners sit around the communion table to receive the Lord's Supper instead. As far as Knox was concerned, this was the closest equivalent to the scriptural account of the Last Supper, and for Knox, any departure from Scripture in the practice of worship was to commit idolatry.

The problem was that with the official acceptance of the prayer book, obedience to the King and the government of the realm now *required* kneeling to receive communion, even with the Black Rubric as a qualifying statement. What was Knox to do? Should he tell his parishioners to hold firm in their practice of sitting to receive, and so commit civil disobedience? Or should they obey their rulers even though Knox had taught them that to kneel was an idolatrous offense against God?!

Since the issue of how the church should respond to the state will be a tremendously significant one over the course of Knox's life, it is worth looking briefly at the letter of advice he sent to his parishioners in Berwick on this very question.[2] In it, he urged deference to the authorities, and so submission to the requirement to kneel because the "common order" should not be overturned "for

ceremonies or rites, things of smaller weight." Since it is very clear that the last thing that Knox personally thought was that details of worship practice were minor matters, and he passionately opposed this one in particular, why was he urging obedience? The answer lies partly in that the rubric had gone some way to meeting his concerns, but also that he had hopes for a more thoroughgoing reform from England's genuinely Protestant government. In the hoped-for big picture, such matters as kneeling at communion were temporary stepping stones on the way, rather than permanent stumbling blocks. So Knox asked his flock at Berwick to kneel for the time being, "for uniform order to be kept."

To Flee or Not to Flee?

Meanwhile, probably in an attempt to render him less vocal in his criticism of the nature and pace of reform—and to bring him nearer to London, where the authorities could keep a closer eye on him—Knox was offered the bishopric of Rochester. He refused it. There is no evidence that he objected to the church having bishops as such, but he certainly did not wish to submit himself to the restrictions a bishopric would impose on what he considered to be his primary vocation of preaching. Knox returned to his preaching ministry in Newcastle, when, in early 1553, he was astonished to discover that he had been appointed vicar of All Hallows Church in London. He refused this as well. Knox was then summoned to London once again and called to the Privy Council to be questioned both about his preaching and about his refusal to accept positions within the church. The Privy Council apparently expressed regret that he was not satisfied with the "common order" established in the English church, to which Knox responded, in typically blunt fashion, that he was all the more sorry that the "common order" established in the English church was contrary to the institution of Jesus Christ!

By this time, Knox knew, as did many, that Edward VI was ailing. He died on July 6, 1553, at the age of 16. In a desperate, dramatic, and tragic attempt to ensure a Protestant succession, he stipulated that his first cousin once removed, Lady Jane Grey, was to be queen, rather than his Roman Catholic half-sister Mary Tudor. Lady Jane is sometimes called the "Nine Days Queen" because she reigned only from the tenth of July until Mary Tudor was proclaimed the rightful Queen on the nineteenth of July. Lady Jane was executed in February the following year, at the age of 16 or 17.

Knox's response to the accession of Mary Tudor was typically blunt: "After the death of this most virtuous Prince [Edward VI], of whom the godless people of England for the most part were not worthy, Satan intended nothing less than that the light of Jesus Christ utterly to have been extinguished . . . for after him was raised up . . . that idolatress Jezebel . . . Mary . . . cruel persecutrix of God's people."[3]

Knox was one of the many prominent Protestants in England who made the agonizing decision to flee to continental Europe as refugees and exiles, rather than to remain in England, with the prospect of severe persecution and perhaps death. He reached Dieppe in 1554, and from there he wrote letters to his former congregations, urging steadfast refusal to compromise with Roman Catholicism. You will find more about the content of these letters in the third key texts section. For the moment, though, the letters seem to have had less effect on his former congregations than the possibility of persecution. It seems that many in Berwick renounced their

Protestant profession. Not Elizabeth and Marjorie Bowes, however, the indomitable mother and daughter of Norham Castle. They remained extremely keen and vocal Protestants, to the extreme irritation of their staunchly Roman Catholic husband and father, Richard Bowes.

A Thwarted Marriage

When Knox left England, he also left behind his fiancée, Marjorie, after many attempts to make the necessary arrangements for their marriage over the preceding year. He and Marjorie were betrothed in 1553, when she was about seventeen and Knox was thirty-eight. Richard Bowes, who was not exactly thrilled with the effect John Knox had had on his wife and daughter, did everything he could to stall matters. He had been very far from impressed by the engagement in the first place, but it appears that both Elizabeth and Marjorie managed to persuade him to accept it. Even so, he was the reverse of cooperative in furthering the arrangements once Knox was summoned south to preach and to be questioned by the Privy Council in 1553. Knox returned northward again as soon as he could in an attempt to finalize matters, knowing that Edward was unlikely to survive much longer and that his death would render Knox's position precarious. Richard Bowes was equally well aware that Mary Tudor would shortly ascend the throne and, needless to say, this made him even less keen on a marriage between one of his daughters and a notorious firebrand of a Protestant preacher. Knox was summoned south again to preach before he could make any further headway.

It was during this preaching tour that Edward died and we find Knox preaching strongly against Roman Catholicism in London as Mary begins her reign. She immediately

issued a proclamation that all preachers must obtain a special license. Many Protestant clergy rapidly found themselves imprisoned, and others fled into exile. Knox, now in considerable danger, made one last secret journey northward to see Elizabeth and Marjorie and to finalize the marriage. He was only able to reach Newcastle, and Richard had forbidden Elizabeth and Marjorie to have any contact with him. Richard's brother, Sir Robert Bowes, was likewise a firm supporter of Mary Tudor and the restoration of Roman Catholicism, and between them, they were determined to prevent the marriage. Indeed, Sir Robert's response when Knox sought to declare his heart in an attempt to persuade him to support the marriage was so disdainful that Knox wrote to Elizabeth that his "despiteful words have so pierced my heart that life is bitter unto me."[4]

So Knox turned back and reached Dieppe without a wife, and racked with doubt and guilt about his decision to leave England for the poverty but safety of exile. From there he made his way to Geneva armed with a lot of questions about theology and politics for John Calvin.

Key Texts 2

The Idolatry
of the Roman Catholic Mass

If you remember, once Knox was released from his time as a French galley slave he took up his calling in England, where he was sent to Northumberland to try to instill

Protestantism in what was considered to be a particularly recalcitrant Roman Catholic corner of the land. You might also recall that he aroused the ire of the staunchly Roman Catholic Bishop of Durham, so that in 1550, he was summoned to defend his preaching and, in particular, his preaching against the Mass, before the Council of the North. Knox published his argument later that year as a tract with the typically forthright title, *A Vindication of the Doctrine That the Sacrifice of the Mass Is Idolatry.* This is our second key text and the first that is wholly by Knox, since the first was his reflections on and adaptation of Balnaves's treatise on justification.

Knox structures his case against the Roman Catholic understanding of the Mass around two blunt syllogisms. The first is that "all worshiping, honoring or service invented by the brain of man in the religion of God, without his express commandment, is idolatry. The Mass is invented by the brain of man without any commandment of God; therefore it is idolatry." The second is similar: "All honoring, or service to God, whereunto is added a wicked

opinion, is abomination. Unto the Mass is added a wicked opinion. Therefore it is abomination."

These might not be the most subtle of syllogisms, and Knox may have used at least as much rhetoric as careful logic in making his case through them, but the structure serves mainly as an ironic platform for Knox to launch his wide-ranging (if somewhat repetitive) attacks. It is ironic because syllogistic logic was the cornerstone of scholasticism, the theological method of the medieval church. Knox was attempting to turn the scholastic method to the service of a Protestant attack on the heart of Roman Catholic piety and practice.

As his attack unfolds, we see that he brings together some characteristic features that we have already noted and that will be central throughout his life. The first is an insistence that all forms of worship must have scriptural warrant. We have seen an example of his willingness to stand up for what he thinks is wrong in this regard in the "Black Rubric" affair, with his strong objections to the practice of kneeling to receive communion. For Knox, God has indicated how he wishes to be worshiped in the Scriptures, and we must not go beyond what we find there by adding ideas of our own. If we do, we are committing idolatry because idolatry is not just worshiping something or someone that is not God, it is worshiping the true God falsely. The second very typical characteristic of Knox that is on display here is his decided preference for drawing on Old Testament examples. Both of these come together in one of his arguments for the first syllogism, when he equates the Roman Catholic rite of the Mass with Saul's disobedience to God in 1 Samuel 15. This is a rather unpleasant episode that includes both Saul's disobedience to a command of God and also his taking it upon himself to offer worship in ways not commanded by God. Just like Saul's blunder here, says Knox, the Mass is an act of idolatry because it interposes human ideas of how God is to be worshiped rather than sticking with how he has asked us to worship him.

As an indication that idolatry in general is as much of a concern as the particular instance of it that he sees in the Mass (and also that he has so many problems with Roman Catholicism that he finds it hard to keep to the main point!) Knox digresses to mention a vast array of Roman Catholic practices critiqued by all Protestants, from the requirement for priestly celibacy to prayers to the saints, all of which he considers to be human inventions rather than being warranted in Scripture. Returning to the Mass, he maintains that none of the theological ideas and elaborate ceremonies that have accrued to the celebration of the sacrament have their basis in the Bible. They are, to return to his syllogism, "invented by the brain of man," and so are idolatrous. He thinks that they foster superstition rather than true worship

of God, something not helped by the fact that the liturgy of the Mass was also in Latin and was therefore incomprehensible to the majority of hearers. To Knox, the focus of Roman Catholic worship was therefore an idolatrous ritual rather than a clear presentation of the gospel. The fieriness of the language is typical of Knox, and the points being made are typical of all Protestant objections to the Mass.

Since the second syllogism is very similar to the first, it is no surprise that Knox essentially repeats many of the same points. Here is the place, though, where he also launches his specific doctrinal attacks, raising objections that once again he shares with all Protestants against the theology of the Mass. Above all, he speaks out against the notion of the Mass as in any way a sacrifice of Christ to the Father. For this to make sense we need to think again about the concept of transubstantiation, mentioned briefly in chapter 1. At the heart of the Roman Catholic understanding of what is happening in the sacrament of the Mass is the notion that at the words of consecration, the substance, or inner essence, of the bread and wine is transformed into the body and blood of Christ, even though the accidents (their outward appearance and how they are perceived by the bodily senses) remain the same. Knox, like all Protestant reformers, rejected the doctrine of transubstantiation and any suggestion that the celebration of the sacrament might be thought of as a reoffering of Christ's sacrifice back to the Father. The Mass was understood, at a crude and a theologically sophisticated level, as at the very least a re-presentation of the sacrifice of Christ upon the cross. For a wonderful artistic depiction of this, take a look at Rogier Van Der Weyden's stunning *Triptych of the Seven Sacraments.* The painting is set in a cathedral, and the left and right panels show the other six sacraments of the Roman Catholic Church in the aisles and side chapels of the cathedral. The main panel is set in the nave—the large central aisle of the cathedral. You will see, in the background, a priest with his back to you raising the host (the communion bread, or wafer) at the moment of consecration and, in the foreground, in a direct sightline to the raised host, the massive figure of Christ on the cross. This painting is from the century before Knox and the Reformation, but there could be no clearer depiction of the quite literal centrality of the Mass in Roman Catholic piety, practice, and thinking before, during, and after the Reformation period than this magnificent work of art.

This way of understanding the Mass, with transubstantiation and sacrifice as its twin pillars, meant that each celebration of it could be understood as an act of propitiation,

pleasing to God the Father and contributing to the forgiveness of sins. In the Council of Trent we find a very trenchant statement that the Mass should be performed often, for the living and the dead, as a sacrifice in which Christ is offered anew to the Father in propitiation: "For inasmuch as in this divine sacrifice which is celebrated in the mass is contained and immolated in an unbloody manner the same Christ who once offered himself in a bloody manner on the altar of the cross; the holy council teaches that this is truly propitiatory. . . . Appeased by this sacrifice, the Lord grants the grace and gift of penitence, and pardons even the gravest crimes and sins. . . . Wherefore, according to the tradition of the Apostles, it is rightly offered not only for the sins, punishments [and] satisfactions . . . of the faithful who are living, but also for those who are departed in Christ but not as yet fully purified."[5]

It has to be said that Knox and other Protestant Reformers were not in the least interested in any subtle theological distinctions that sought to qualify the idea that the Mass was in some way a "repetition" of Christ's saving sacrifice on the cross. To a Protestant, transubstantiation and an understanding of the Mass that included the idea that it was in some way propitiatory undermined the once-for-all sacrifice of Christ. Likewise, any suggestion of the priest offering Christ or his sacrifice back to the Father was also seen as undermining the idea of Christ alone as High Priest in his once-for-all self-offering on the cross.

Knox (along with other Protestants) therefore considered the Mass to be idolatrous because the Roman Catholic doctrine of transubstantiation led to worship of the bread and the wine as if they were Christ himself, offered back to God the Father in a sacrificial act by the priest. This in turn led directly to what he considered to be the superstitious use of the sacrament because of it being seen as a "good work" that contributed directly to salvation. Since the sacrament is pleasing to God, it was assumed that the more frequently it was performed, the more pleased God would be. This was the basis for the practice of saying masses for various circumstances (for a good harvest, for example, or for peace) and also for the practice, as hinted at in the quotation above, of paying for masses for the souls of those who had died and were in purgatory, where, as the name implies, people continued to be purged of their sins until they were eventually admitted into heaven.[6] In other words, to return to the theme of the previous key text, the Mass was seen as one of the works that would help you to be justified—to be set right with God—in this life and also in the next. In addition to attending Mass as often as you could—and perhaps once a year actually receiving the bread (you wouldn't ever receive the wine as that was only for the priests)—you would want to have as many masses as possible said for you

after you had died, to help you get out of purgatory. So, if you had the money, you made provision in your will for as many masses to be said for you as you could afford and you hoped that your friends and relatives would have as many masses said for you as they could afford as well.

Not surprisingly, if you were a Protestant, and so considered that Scripture taught that human beings are justified only by grace through faith, then you thought that the Roman Catholic understanding of the Mass was another form of justification by works on top of everything else you felt was wrong about it. Therefore you spoke out against it as often and as strongly as you could. You also recognized that the Mass was the most important expression of someone's faith and spirituality and self-understanding as a Roman Catholic. So, if you could demonstrate that both the way that Mass was celebrated and the thinking behind it were wrong, then you had dismantled the foundations of Roman Catholicism for most people. This is one of the reasons why Knox, and many others, spent so much time passionately preaching and arguing against it.

Knox makes it very clear that for him the Mass was the foremost demonstration of how a false theology insufficiently based in Scripture led to false worship that also departed from Scripture, which led in turn to more false theology. While we might find Knox's blunt, strident approach distasteful, that is how all sides engaged in theological disputes in the sixteenth century. There is nothing particularly distinctive about the objections Knox raises or the way he expresses them either. All of this and more had been standard fare since the outset of the Reformation. What we do find in this tract, though, is Knox's distinctive public voice: pugnacious, fiery, rhetorical, always more of a preacher than a precise theological debater. As we will see in chapter 6, when he deals with private spiritual problems his tone is

markedly different, but for the moment this is an example of Knox the prophet of God, thundering against what he consider to be the false and idolatrous church of Rome.

Key Texts 3

Public Letters to England, 1554

With the restoration of Roman Catholicism after the accession of Mary Tudor in 1553, everything seemed to fall apart for the Protestant cause in England. From his exile, Knox made up for his physical absence with powerful letters to his former congregations and to the nation of England (our key texts here) and with his infamous *First Blast of the Trumpet against the Monstrous Regiment of Women* (key text 4). It is with these documents that we begin to see the overt

intertwining of the theological and the political in Knox's writing as the changing situations in England (and later in Scotland) push him toward evermore radical positions with regard to the theological justification for resistance to and rebellion against a ruler.

The "Godly Letter"

Already, on the eve of his exile in 1554, Knox had begun to write what is known as the Godly Letter, which is addressed to his former congregations in Northumberland.[7] He completed it shortly after he set foot on French soil, before heading to Geneva. His intention was to shore up their courage to refuse to attend the reinstated Roman Catholic Mass. The title page set the tone: "He that continueth to the end shall be saved" (see Matt. 10:22). The basic argument was simple, and it is similar to key text 2: the Mass is idolatry and God will punish idolaters. His congregation members ought to fear God more than they fear any earthly rulers and to obey God's laws rather than a monarch's ungodly decrees.

In this sermon-letter we see both of the key themes already noted in Knox's writing: his hatred of what he considers to be idolatry and also the importance of the Old Testament prophets. He identifies Mary Tudor immediately with Jezebel, the Baal-worshiping queen who opposes the prophet Elijah (see 1 Kgs. 18). In this letter, though, it is the prophet Jeremiah who dominates. Knox makes constant and direct parallels between the situation of Judah at the time of Jeremiah and that of England, maintaining that England is in fact "worse than unthankful Judah," and so is even more deserving of God's judgment because of turning back again so quickly to the idolatry of the Mass and not heeding or helping the supporters of the Protestant cause. He compares the Mass directly to the idolatrous worship of Baal that was one of the reasons for God's wrath against Judah in Jeremiah 11, and he argues that even in Jeremiah's time, there was more support for the prophet and his unwelcome message than for the true gospel in England under Mary Tudor.

Jeremiah serves not only as an interpretative tool for Knox but also as an example. Knox utters his own prophecies for England based on the pattern found in Jeremiah, in which there are warnings of the certainty of dire punishment to be inflicted by God if the people continue to disobey but there is also the promise of mercy, healing, and restoration if the people repent. This twofold pattern of preaching in fact becomes known as a "jeremiad" and is immensely popular with later Puritan preachers. Since Knox did not hold out much hope that the people of England would repent, he prophesied that "London would be made a desert" under the rule of Mary Tudor, just as Jeremiah had predicted the destruction of Jerusalem. Jeremiah therefore becomes the key both to Knox's interpretation of the present situation in England and also to his self-understanding in his role as a Protestant prophet.

In terms of how his former congregations should respond, Knox is clear at this stage that their task is to take whatever steps necessary to keep themselves from idolatry, either by going into exile or by refusing to participate in the Mass no matter what the consequences. His former flock is not to submit to the idolatrous demands of Mary Tudor and her government, but theirs is to be passive resistance to a government inflicted on England by God as a punishment for the nation's lack of wholehearted commitment to the gospel and refusal to heed the warnings of prophetic voices such as his.

The "Faithful Admonition . . ."

In May of 1554 Knox wrote two more public letters to the Protestants of England—"Comfortable Epistles to His Afflicted Brethren." In these he sought to comfort English Protestants, to strengthen their resolve, and to assure them of God's judgment on those oppressing them. He also insisted that they were not to presume to take vengeance into their own hands, but to leave this to God and instead to pray for their persecutors. Less than two months later, though, it became clear that Mary was beginning to take much harsher measures against Protestant believers and that she would make refusal to attend and partake of Mass an act of treason, punishable by death. Although the figures aren't clear, it is agreed that around three hundred Protestants were burned at the stake during her five-year reign. Although the burnings had not yet begun, Knox's tone changed.

So, in July 1554, he writes his *Faithful Admonition to the Professors of God's Truth in England*.[8] He first urges Protestants to stand firm and to trust in God, both for their personal salvation and for the future of England. He then rebukes those hypocrites who attend Mass with mental equivocations in order to avoid the persecution that an open profession of Protestantism would bring. Finally, he closes with savage imprecations against Mary Tudor and her leading councilors. She was worse than Jezebel, and her councilors were worse than she, for forcing people to participate in the idolatry of the Mass. In by far the most violent language he had so far used, he quite literally wishes them all dead and in hell, and prays as such, borrowing the language of the Psalms: "Repress the pride of those blood-thirsty tyrants; consume them in thine anger . . . pour forth thy vengeance, O Lord! . . . let death devour them . . . let them go down quick to the hell." Even more audaciously, he prays fervently for God to raise up a Jehu "to execute [God's] just judgments against idolaters." If you look up 2 Kings 9–10, you will see what Knox is referring to here, especially the assassination of Jezebel at the end of 2 Kings 9. In other words, Knox is longing for someone to be called by God to assassinate Mary Tudor—tyrant, idolatress, and oppressor of God's people.

While Knox's language in the *Faithful Admonition* was extremely violent, the views behind the language were as yet quite moderate in comparison to what some were beginning to advocate. As we will see in the next chapter, these letters reflect the theological and political caution of

Heinrich Bullinger, whom Knox consulted for help on such matters, albeit expressed in vitriolic, imprecatory prayer. There is no call here for other members of the ruling class or nobility to instigate a rebellion against Mary, for example, still less for the people as a whole to take this upon themselves. God's people are to confine themselves to passive resistance. They are to refuse to participate in idolatrous practices—even though this refusal has now become an act of treason—and to bear the consequences, entrusting themselves to the faithfulness of God and hoping that God would raise up a deliverer for the nation.

CHAPTER THREE

A Turbulent Exile

When he reached Geneva, Knox delighted in Calvin's preaching and pretty much got straight down to business, seeking Calvin's advice about the theological and political issues weighing on his mind. These mostly related to whether women could rule and whether subjects had the right to rebel against an ungodly ruler. Because of the importance of these questions for what Knox does and writes during this period of his life, we're going to follow him by plunging straight into his quest for answers.

Though Calvin never put his specific response to the issues Knox raised with him in writing—they could, after all, discuss everything face-to-face—we know from his own writings up to this time that his answers would have been discouraging to Knox. With regard to women rulers,

Calvin's view was that on the whole they were a bad thing and likely to be a punishment from God for a nation's sins. The biblical example of Deborah (Judg. 4–5) was the exception that proved the rule. Deborah was a successful ruler over Israel in the period when Israel was ruled by judges, before Israel demanded to be ruled by a king. But Calvin would have been reluctant to offer any incentive for developing a theological rationale for active resistance against a ruler, even an ungodly woman ruler, which is what Knox was clearly hoping for. Perhaps sensing Knox's disappointment (or impatient with his persistence!), Calvin encouraged him to write to other leading theologians too, namely Heinrich Bullinger in Zurich and Pierre Viret in Lausanne, for further wisdom on the matters he had raised.

Although he put other questions to Bullinger too, here are the main lines of Knox's most important questions for our purposes, and also the main lines of Bullinger's rather cautious responses:

> **Knox:** Can a woman rule over a kingdom and then transfer the right of sovereignty to her husband if she marries?

> **Bullinger:** Well . . . even though divine law requires that women be subject to men, if the law of the land allows a woman to be the head of state, then the law of the land must be accepted. As for the transfer of sovereignty issue . . . refer to the law of the land in question.

(At the forefront of Knox's mind here was the impending marriage between Mary Tudor and Philip of Spain, which had been one of the catalysts for an abortive rebellion in England. You can see how his mind was working. The implicit question behind Knox's question was whether a

possible transfer of sovereignty might be justification enough for launching a major rebellion. And Bullinger wasn't going to answer it.)

> **Knox:** Should rulers who enforce idolatry and condemn true religion be obeyed, and could other members of the ruling classes defend themselves against them?

> **Bullinger:** Under *no* circumstances should anyone give obedience to commands that oppose God's revealed will in Scripture, no matter what the consequences of disobedience. BUT under most circumstances, that should be passive resistance. There doesn't seem to be any biblical warrant for rebellion against a ruler. *However* . . . the Lord does sometimes raise up individuals to enact his justice on unjust rulers. Jehoiada is one example, among others.

(You can look up 2 Kgs. 11 to see what Bullinger is referring to with this example.)

Knox: Should the common people obey members of the ruling class who rebel or the idolatrous sovereign?

Bullinger: Well, since there really shouldn't be any rebellion of any kind against a ruler this is a moot point. But it really does depend on circumstances. Maybe there could be *some* circumstances when it could be legitimate . . . but it's better to wait for God's deliverance than try to anticipate how that might come about.

What Knox received from Bullinger, then, was a very cautious admission that Scripture holds out the possibility of an extraordinary act of deliverance from God, but no encouragement at all to develop a theological justification for rebellion. In the last of our key texts we saw that, for all the violence of Knox's language, this is the position that is reflected in his 1554 public letters to England. Although we have no record of Viret's response, from other works of his we can surmise that Knox might have received somewhat more encouragement to keep thinking about other possibilities. Viret is clear that resistance against ungodly tyrants is justifiable. It must be passive at first, and then if all other routes have been tried, and if led by other members of the ruling class, rebellion. Moreover, this is justifiable simply in the case of political tyranny as well as religious persecution. Where religious persecution is involved, he is clear that magistrates have a *duty* not just a right to depose a tyrant who threatens the cause of the gospel.[1]

All this gave Knox much to ponder, and we will see the fruits of his developing views in the next chapter. In the meanwhile, though, he traveled from Geneva back to Dieppe, seeking the latest news from England and Scotland

and hoping to slip across the Channel to marry Marjorie at long last. That proved to be impossible, so he returned to Geneva again, longing for some peace in order to study and write. Instead, he received a letter from the English exiles in Frankfurt, asking him to be one of their pastors. Though he was reluctant, Calvin persuaded him to go.

Prayerbooks in Frankfurt and Preaching in Scotland

Knox arrived in late 1554, and for a turbulent few months he found himself in the midst of a church torn apart by bitter disputes about which service book to use. They were using a modified version of the 1552 *Book of Common Prayer*, with some elements taken out (including some of the set prayers and responses, the command to kneel at communion, and the requirement for ministers to wear particular vestments). However, some of the exiles wanted to use the 1552 *Book of Common Prayer* exactly as it was, partly out of conviction and also partly out of loyalty to its primary author, Thomas Cranmer, shortly to be burned at the stake under Mary Tudor. Still others in the congregation wanted to use an English translation of the order of worship used in Geneva. Perhaps surprisingly, Knox was extraordinarily diplomatic in all of this, trying for months to bring the warring factions together, but several fresh influxes of English exiles, all strongly committed to the 1552 *Book of Common Prayer*, tipped the balance. Knox lost this particular battle, thanks to a great deal of church politics and wider politics too; those who opposed Knox drew his *Faithful Admonition*, with its fierce rhetoric about resisting rulers, to the attention of Frankfurt's government. That helped to encourage these rulers to get rid of him. Knox and his followers were forced out in March 1555. All sides had been keeping Calvin up to date with the issues and trying to win him over to their point of view. In a letter to those chiefly responsible for throwing Knox and his followers out, he wrote tersely that, in his view, Knox was not dealt with in a godly or brotherly fashion. Calvin was of the opinion that it would have been better that some of their number had remained in England rather than come to cause division among the exiles.[2]

Once again we find Knox setting off for Geneva, and once again he wasn't there for long. Some news reached him from Scotland, and it was unexpectedly good. Unlike the violent persecution in England, Mary of Guise, whom we last met in chapter 1 (the widow of James V and mother of Mary, Queen of Scots), was now Regent of Scotland and seemed to be showing considerable openness to Protestantism. Things were looking promising, and Knox was asked to return. He arrived in Edinburgh in September

1555 and spent the next seven months or so traveling around Scotland, staying with and preaching in the houses of Protestant gentry and being visited by many of the leading political figures. As Roger Mason has pointed out, the greatest impact Knox had on this occasion was not in gaining new converts from Roman Catholicism—he preached only among gathered groups of committed Protestants— but in helping to galvanize the Scottish Protestant movement by establishing contact with and between key noblemen with Protestant sympathies.[3] Knox's preaching tour did much to lay the foundations of Protestantism as a revolutionary political force. This would bear fruit later when many of those whom Knox met at this time would become the Lords of the Congregation, the group who would overthrow Mary of Guise and establish Protestantism in Scotland.

Knox's preaching seemed as though it was about to come to an abrupt end in May 1556, however, when he was summoned to Edinburgh on a charge of heresy. Most people who received such a summons slipped quietly away. Knox called their bluff and entered Edinburgh openly the day before the heresy commission was due to sit. After all her attempts to placate the Protestants, the last thing the regent wanted was John Knox on trial. She put pressure on the heresy commission, and the charges were dropped on a technicality. Knox then preached publicly in Edinburgh for the next couple of weeks. He had realized by this stage, however, that Mary of Guise's leniency toward Protestantism was likely to be short lived. Her intention had simply been to raise the widest possible support for the marriage of her daughter, the child-queen Mary, to the heir to the French throne. Since her apparent openness to Protestants was a matter of temporary expediency rather than offering the prospect of a settled policy, there was little further point—and very great danger—in Knox remaining in Scotland for much longer. He returned to Geneva to be one of the pastors to the exiled English community there. Almost as soon as he left, he was indicted for heresy in his absence and burned in effigy.

When he returned to Geneva it was as a married man at last, accompanied by his wife, Marjorie, and also by his mother-in-law, Elizabeth. The details aren't clear, but it seems as though, rather than Knox attempting to resolve the issues by going to Northumberland, Marjorie and Elizabeth might have joined Knox in Edinburgh, and Knox and Marjorie might have been married there. Not long after the wedding, as Knox was winding up his trip to Scotland, he had a last-minute invitation to meet with another potentially influential nobleman, so he arranged for Marjorie and

Elizabeth to set sail ahead of him for Dieppe and wait for him there. When he joined them, they spent a few weeks there together before setting off for Geneva.

We are left to speculate as to how Richard Bowes felt about the departure of his wife as well as his daughter. It was not altogether unusual for Protestant husbands to send their wives and children to the continent for their safety. So, for example, Knox's friend Henry Lock sent his wife, Anne, and their children to Geneva, and Knox himself had urged her strongly to come. Perhaps the Roman Catholic Richard Bowes might have consoled himself with the thought that at least Elizabeth and Marjorie would be safe, and he would be rid of the embarrassment of their uncompromising, high-profile Protestantism. We will turn to the complexities of Knox's relationships with Elizabeth Bowes and Anne Lock in chapter 6.

The Good Life in Geneva

For the moment, Knox now seemed to be well settled in Geneva. He was pastor to a community of around 150 English exiles, many of whom were prominent scholars and theologians. The congregation included the remarkable group of men, some of whom had been Knox's allies in Frankfurt, who produced the Geneva Bible: William Whittingham, Anthony Gilby, Miles Coverdale, Christopher Goodman, Thomas Sampson, and William Cole. The Geneva Bible was the first Bible in English to have verse numbers (the standard verse numbers that we all know now for the New Testament were only introduced in 1551) and also the first generally accessible English Bible to have significant aids to interpretation, such as some very substantial marginal notes. In effect it was a "study Bible." The Geneva Bible New Testament and the Psalms came out in 1557 and the first full Bible, with a revised version of the New Testament, in 1560. It went through many editions, with changes to the marginal notes, and it was the version that all households in Scotland with sufficient means were required by law to purchase in 1579.[4]

Calvin found Geneva to be endlessly troublesome, but to Knox it was, as he famously put it, "the most perfect school of Christ that ever was on earth since the days of the Apostles."[5] Knox had a much less turbulent time as pastor of the English church there than in Frankfurt, and it is clear that his wife, Marjorie, was a considerable help and support to him. She was an educated woman, able to act as his secretary, and was widely admired, including by Calvin, for her gracious charm as a hostess as well as her intellectual abilities. The Knoxes were a popular couple. Elizabeth, too, was a tremendous help in setting Marjorie free from some of her domestic duties in order to be of more assistance to Knox

in his work. Marjorie gave birth to their first son, Nathaniel, in 1557, and a second son, Eleazer, in 1558.

Knox didn't get long to enjoy being a father, though. Shortly after Nathaniel entered the world, Knox received a letter suggesting that he should return to Scotland, intimating that the Protestant gentry were about to rise in rebellion. When he reached Dieppe, he found further letters indicating that those who had contemplated the uprising had dropped the whole idea. Knox was furious, both at having been put to so much trouble himself and at the apparent backing down of the nobles in the face of Mary of Guise. He wrote back sharply to them, saying that they should have been prepared to "vindicate and deliver your subjects and brethren from all violence and oppression to the uttermost of your power."[6] He then made his way back to

Geneva to work in earnest on the combination of Scripture, theology, and politics that would lead him to his first major published work and then on two very significant tracts that would set the stage for the next phase of his life and for the next episode in the history of Scotland.

Clarion Calls to Rebellion

We have seen that his years in exile have largely been preoccupied with matters related to the situation in Scotland and also the controversy surrounding the church for English exiles in Frankfurt. In 1557, however, he once again turned his full fury—and his latest thinking on the relationship between theology and politics—against Mary Tudor, Queen of England. The result was perhaps his most famous, and definitely his most infamous book: *The First Blast of the Trumpet against the Monstrous Regiment of Women.*[7]

Since language has changed, a little clarification about the title might be in order. If you are going to be offended by it, and you probably will be, you at least need to know what he means. Knox did not have in mind some sort of monstrous army of women. The word *regiment* here means "rule," and the word *monstrous* has stronger connotations of "unnatural" than we would associate with it today. So, what Knox is setting out to do here is make the case that it is unnatural (although also, in his view, monstrous in the sense that we still use that word!) for women to be in political authority. This exposes the irony that in the sixteenth century, there was no other societal role in which women could officially have authority over men apart from the highest rank of all.

The *First Blast* was published anonymously in Geneva in 1558, but it didn't take long for everyone to work out that Knox was the author. Even for a notoriously fiery writer and preacher, it was explosive, both for its ideas and for the violence with which they were expressed. It provoked a storm of controversy from the outset, although not necessarily for the reasons that people find it offensive today. As we'll see when we take a closer look at it in the next key texts section, it wasn't so much his views on women rulers that caused outrage from his contemporaries, as it was his views on the right of subjects to rebel.

As it happened, though, Knox's timing was appalling. The book had barely been published when Mary Tudor died, and the Protestant Elizabeth I became Queen of England. She was very well aware of Knox's book and was very decidedly *not* amused. Her situation was precarious enough, without this notorious book attempting to deny the legitimacy of all women rulers and promoting the right to rebellion. Knox's attempt to mend fences was extremely clumsy and totally unsuccessful. He wrote to William Cecil, Elizabeth's Secretary of State, to say that as long as Elizabeth acknowledged that her legitimacy as a ruler derived from her having been raised up by God as his special instrument rather than being on the basis of heredity, he would have no objections to her rule at all. It is doubtful whether Cecil ever even showed Elizabeth the letter. The moment that Elizabeth became Queen, there was a chorus of voices from among the English exiles in Geneva writing or speaking against the *First Blast*. Even Calvin felt the need to write to Cecil about it, trying to distance himself from the views expressed in it. Queen Elizabeth's relations with Calvin were poisoned from the start by Knox's book, printed by one of Geneva's most prominent publishing houses, and it remained one of the many reasons why she was always deeply suspicious of the exiles who returned to England from there.

While the *First Blast* was controversial enough, Knox was already beginning to move toward an even more radical

position than he articulated there, as he turned once again to address the increasingly volatile situation in Scotland. Back in 1556, during his preaching tour there, Knox had written what was, for him, a rather mild, relatively conciliatory letter to the regent, Mary of Guise. As we've seen, at that stage it seemed as though for political reasons, even if not out of personal conviction, she might take a reasonably generous attitude toward the Protestants among her subjects. At that point, Knox had had the good sense to moderate his usual hectoring tone in the hopes of persuading her to further concessions. Apparently she brushed the letter off with a laugh when she received it, and by 1558, with young Queen Mary safely married to the heir to the French throne, she no longer had any need to win the support of the Protestant nobles. So she began to look less favorably on Protestantism in general. Everyone sensed that the velvet gloves were coming off, and Knox's tone changed accordingly.

First, he wrote a revised version of his 1556 letter to the regent, emphasizing that the civil authorities had the right to reform the church if the church would not reform itself (an important aspect of the mainstream Reformation movement, strongly articulated early on in Martin Luther's 1520 tract, *An Appeal to the German Nobility*). He then ominously pointed out that if elements of the government decided to uphold the church in its corruption rather than seeking to reform it according to the word of God then the people must resist. Moreover, even the lowliest has the right to rebuke a ruler as he, John Knox, was doing in his vocation as a prophet. In that role, he duly threatened her with divine judgment if she should fail to advance the cause of Protestantism in Scotland.

It seems as though she treated this second letter with as much scorn as the first. It was little more than a warning shot across the regent's bows, though. Knox then sent two far more important tracts: his *Appellation to the Nobility* and his *Letter to the Commonality*. In these we see the

clearest statement yet, not only that those who had political power under a monarch had an obligation to overthrow an idolatrous monarch but also that the people had an obligation to rise up in rebellion as well. These twin tracts will be the subject of key texts 5, as Knox's writings become a catalyst that would help to ignite a Protestant revolution in his native land.

Key Texts 4

The First Blast of the Trumpet against the Monstrous Regiment of Women

We now take a closer look at Knox's notorious *First Blast of the Trumpet against the Monstrous Regiment of Women* to help us trace the development of his political theology. Knox's first main point was that he considered the rule of women to be contrary to natural and divine law. He thinks

both make it perfectly clear that, except in the most extraordinary circumstances, women should not have any authority over men, and his assumption is that women are on the whole naturally incapable of wise government anyway. To make his case, he appeals to Scripture, the early church fathers, classical history, and philosophy. Although some theologians were already taking a more generous view of the capacities of women as rulers, Knox's position here is essentially mainstream for his time. Many Protestants and Roman Catholics shared his basic assumptions in this regard, and Knox's overall position is simply a more fiery articulation of the view held by Bullinger in response to the question about the legitimacy of female rule that we noted in the previous chapter. As we saw, Calvin likewise felt that under ordinary circumstances women should not rule over men and that in general a country under the rule of a woman could consider itself under God's judgment, although God might also raise up a godly and heroic woman to rule in a way that is a blessing for God's people. There will be plenty to cause offense to Knox's contemporaries in the *First Blast*, but not his general view about women.

Knox does feel obliged to admit that there have indeed been some good women rulers, since, after all, Scripture indicates as much. Deborah was mentioned in the previous chapter as one such (see Judg. 4–5 for her role as one of the good judges over Israel). Nevertheless, Knox maintains that these are exceptions to the rule and that Mary Tudor is emphatically not such an exception. She is a Jezebel, as we have already seen (1 Kgs. 18) and an Athaliah (2 Kgs. 11). And Scripture is very clear about what needs to be done with such wicked and idolatrous women rulers.

At this point Knox became far more controversial for his time. He argued that not only was it the right, it was also the godly *duty* of the nobility to repress Mary's tyranny with all means at their disposal, up to and including execution. Not to oppose an idolatrous ruler to the death is in fact to rebel against God, to deny the obligations of a covenant relationship with God. The *First Blast* therefore almost totally denies the legitimacy of women monarchs, and it upholds the right to rebellion and regicide when opposition to the monarch is led by other members of the ruling class. It was this theological and scriptural summons to overthrow a ruling monarch, more than his attitude toward women rulers as such, that scandalized many and created problems, not only for Knox but also for Calvin and for the exiles who returned to England from Geneva when Elizabeth became Queen.

In the *First Blast* Knox has therefore moved from a position that advocated total but passive resistance to an unjust and idolatrous monarch (which he maintained in his early letters to his former congregations) to the hope that God might raise up an individual to be the instrument of his vengeance in his *Faithful Admonition* to the people of England. Now he was presenting a rationale to legitimize members of the nobility and ruling class rising up to overthrow an idolatrous, tyrannical monarch. In addition to finding Old Testament warrant for the assassination of ungodly women rulers, his thinking on the concept of covenant is very important. Knox had been gradually developing his ideas about the various covenant relationships within the political order and how these should relate to the covenant between God and his people. Scripture seemed to indicate several kinds of covenants with regard to the ordering of Israel's political life, in addition to the main covenant between God and his people. So, for example, rulers could make covenants with the people, which made them accountable to their people. As always, for Knox, the Old Testament could provide a precise model for the present situation. Could a ruler forfeit the right to obedience from a nation, by either breaking faith with the nation's people or attempting to break the nation's covenant with God? In the time of Edward VI, England became a truly Protestant nation, and so, in Knox's eyes, a nation that had covenanted with God

under the gospel. When a ruler arose who sought to break that bond by returning the nation to Roman Catholicism, that ruler was surely guilty of breaking the covenant made with God. Thus, it became the covenant obligation of the ruling classes to depose and punish such a ruler.

We also see the importance of this concept of covenant in his final public letter to the people of England—his *A Brief Exhortation to England* of 1559, after the death of Mary Tudor. Over and over again he stresses that by submitting to idolatry in Mary Tudor's reign, the nation had broken covenant with God and so deserved God's punishment. Since they have now received a second chance, by the mercy of God, it is the responsibility of God's covenant people to remain faithful themselves and also to hold their rulers to strict account. No edict from a ruler should become a snare to anyone's conscience to lead them to disobey the word of God, and likewise, "If the King himself would usurp any other authority in God's religion than becometh a member of Christ's body" he should be subject to the discipline of the church.[8]

Even though the position Knox came to in the *First Blast* was inflammatory and controversial enough, it was still by no means the most extreme position to hold at the time. In fact, Knox's close friend Christopher Goodman wrote a far more radical tract on the subject, published by the same printing press in Geneva. Goodman and Knox had met in England, and then Goodman became one of Knox's staunchest supporters in the Frankfurt controversy and fellow minister with Knox of the English Church in Geneva. The two men had clearly been thinking together about the theo-political issues raised by Mary Tudor's reign in England, and their two tracts appeared at almost the same time. Goodman's was a much tamer affair in terms of its title and writing style, and so it was and is much less well known. The

title (with modernized spelling) is: *How superior powers ought to be obeyed [by] their subjects: and wherein they may lawfully by God's word be disobeyed and resisted*. Not quite as catchy as *The First Blast of the Trumpet*, but Goodman was actually far more extreme in his views than Knox. Goodman maintained that it was not simply the right and duty of other members of the ruling classes to rebel against a monarch, but it was the right and duty of *every* godly citizen to do as much. In other words, Goodman wrote to give theological and scriptural legitimacy to a popular uprising. While Knox gained most notoriety through his fiery, violent language, his views were moderate in comparison to his friend's, at least at this stage. As we will see in the next key texts section, Knox's thinking continues to develop in response to the changing situation in Scotland, and he comes to articulate a view that is very close to Goodman's.

Key Texts 5

Public Letters to Scotland, 1558

After writing his mistimed attack on Mary Tudor in the *First Blast*, Knox turned his attention back to Scotland and

to twin tracts to help Protestants there recognize what he considered to be their duties as loyal citizens of God's kingdom while under the idolatrous rule of the Roman Catholic Regent Mary of Guise. In his *Appellation to the Nobility*, he made abundantly clear that it was not simply their right but their duty before God to oppose and punish idolatrous rulers. Here we see Knox clearly and forcefully articulating in the Scottish context what he had already maintained in his *First Blast* against Mary Tudor of England: that one sector of the ruling class not only could but should actively rebel against idolatry in another element of the government. For Knox, on the basis of the Old Testament examples of Moses, who disciplined Aaron (as leader of Israel to High Priest), and the reforming kings of Judah and Israel, who purged idolatrous practices from the worship of God, the "civil powers" or political rulers have the obligation to reform and oversee the church. Since God has raised up members of the ruling classes to their position of power and influence, they must show their faithfulness to God in their zeal to uphold and maintain right religion. He goes one step further than in his *First Blast*, however, by also stating that it was the right and duty of *all* the people to support the nobility in their uprising.

As Knox pointed out, if the monarch (or in this case, the regent) had been a truly godly person, there would be no need to appeal to the lesser rulers to take the lead in this regard. Knox is not at all a proto-advocate for democracy, or even anti-monarchy as such. The only issue at stake for him is, how is true religion (read Protestantism) to be established and maintained? Whatever the political system in place, this has to be the priority. When the monarch fails in this duty, then it passes to the next highest civil power, and that happens to be the nobility. It becomes their duty to maintain right religion even to the point of armed rebellion if necessary. Knox issues reminders from texts such as Deuteronomy 13 that those who command idolatry "ought to be punished by death without favour or respect of person."[9] Otherwise, they will be subject to the wrath and punishment of God for regarding earthly rulers more highly than the one Heavenly King. God does not require obedience to rulers whose decrees are against his commands, and he will not spare those who abrogate their duty to oppose them.

Romans 13 is an important text for Knox as he works out his theology of resistance and rebellion, just as it is for other Reformers who took a similar line. Among other things, Romans 13 states that everyone should be subject to the governing authorities because they have been appointed by God to uphold the good and punish wrongdoing, and so to defy them would be to defy God. On the face of it such a text might seem to suggest absolute obedience to whomever

is in power, but the key issue is whether or not the governing authorities are indeed upholding the good—and if not, whether this absolves believers from the duty of obedience. As Acts 5:29 makes clear, disciples of Jesus are always to obey God in preference to the human powers that be whenever there is any clash between what the two require. Along with others such as Viret, however, Knox also interprets Romans 13 as a mandate for the overthrow of wicked rulers. This is because the text suggests that the role of all who have political power should be to uphold what is good in God's sight. Romans 13 therefore becomes a clarion call urging the nobility not to be passive in the face of a ruler's ungodliness. They too are appointed political powers and their task under God is to promote and maintain godliness: "if you be powers ordained by God (and that I hope all men will grant) then by the plain words of the Apostle is the sword given unto you by God for maintenance of the innocent and punishment of malefactors."[10] By extension this also means to "repress the rage and insolency of [monarchs] whensoever they . . . transgress God's blessed ordinance."[11] Interpreted as a text about the obligations of rulers before God rather than the duty of those under them, Romans 13 therefore becomes a text that holds out the possibility of rebellion against a ruler without incurring the wrath of God for disobedience against governing authorities.

The theme of covenant also resurfaces in the *Appellation* as an important one for Knox, just as it had in the *First Blast*. The covenant made between Josiah and God on behalf of the nation to purge the land of idolatry (2 Kgs. 23) becomes the model of the idea of a covenant relationship between God and temporal government, be that the monarch or others to whom the law of the land gives political authority. It is on the basis of this kind of covenant that all rulers are obliged to establish and maintain true religion and to punish idolatry. If the primary rulers of the land do not see themselves bound by such a covenant obligation, other political leaders must act in accordance with it and depose the idolatrous rulers. It is also on the basis of this kind of covenant that subjects have the right to hold their rulers accountable and to resist a ruler who turns from true worship of God to idolatry. This is because all such covenants are ultimately rooted in the one foundational covenant, which is between God and his people and which takes priority over all others.

Exodus 34 becomes Knox's primary text for this argument in the *Appellation* and is the implied basis of the entire argument in the *Letter to the Commonality* to which we will turn in a moment. For Knox, since the covenant with God

binds all people equally, this means both that all people are equally guilty if they passively accept rulers who defy God and that all people are equally responsible for upholding the covenant. As he puts it, "if any go about to erect and set up idolatry or to teach defection from God . . . then not only the magistrates to whom the sword is committed, but also the people are bound by that oath which they have made to God to revenge to the uttermost of their power the injury done against His majesty."[12]

The *Letter to the Commonality* picks up on and extends this theme. We need to note, incidentally, that when Knox refers to the "commonality," he is not referring to all people, or what he refers to as the "rascal multitude."[13] The term "commonality" refers to what we would probably call today the "middle class"—people who had a profession or trade, or people with land and income, but not members of the ruling class. There is some dispute among Knox scholars as to whether or not this letter constitutes a call to popular rebellion. The fact that it can be interpreted in this way at all indicates that Knox is at least hovering on the edge of this position and that a good deal of what he writes here could easily be interpreted as inciting an uprising.

For the first time, Knox addresses this group of people and insists that they too have the right and obligation not only to refuse to obey idolatrous rulers but to hold their rulers to account and, it would seem, to rebel if necessary. Knox is clear that what he requires of the regent and the nobility he also requires of the members of the commonality—that they do everything in their power to establish and uphold the true worship of God. While all may not be equal in the political hierarchy, all are equal when it comes to their standing before God. God has made this covenant with all believers, and there is nothing more important to believers than to walk in obedience to their covenant obligations. They must uphold and defend these to the uttermost.

Obedience to God therefore might well entail defying and rebelling against those to whom, under ordinary circumstances, political obedience is due. In a splendid example of his fiery eloquence, he states that

> if (as God forbid) . . . the fear of your princes and the wisdom of the world draw you back from God and from His Son Christ Jesus, be ye certainly persuaded that ye shall drink the cup of his vengeance. . . . It will not excuse you (dear Brethren) in the presence of God . . . to say, "We were but simple subjects; we could not redress the faults and crimes of our rulers. . . . We called for reformation, and wished for the same . . . but were compelled to give obedience to all that they demanded." These vain excuses, I say, will nothing avail you in the presence of God.[14]

As was the case in his letter to the nobility, Knox then issued stark reminders that *all people* who simply submitted to idolatrous rulers and their decrees would be treated equally by God as themselves idolaters and blasphemers.

Knox makes the right of all subjects to have true gospel preachers (in other words, Protestant ministers) an important touchstone for whether rulers are meeting their covenant obligations and also whether the people are meeting theirs. Not only must all people do what it takes to see that false preachers are removed and true preachers are established, they must also defend those preachers by all means necessary against any persecution and danger, even if that means defying their social and political superiors. We will see in the next chapter that the uprising that will lead to the establishment of Protestantism in Scotland begins exactly

this way, as some of the nobility and commonality band together to defend their Protestant preachers from the regent's threats against them.

Perhaps it might be best to say that rather than an appeal to instigate an uprising "from below," Knox's *Letter to the Commonality* taken together with his *Appellation to the Nobility* expressed the hope that the nobles would initiate a rebellion and the commonality would recognize their duty to support the nobles against the regent and the Roman Catholic Church. However, taken together with a book that was never published, but of which Knox wrote a very clear draft, we can see that he was preparing to make a case for the radical position espoused earlier by his friend Christopher Goodman.

This is because Knox added an appendix to the *Appellation to the Nobility* and the *Letter to the Commonality*. It was a draft of what would have been the sequel to the *First Blast*. It was quite literally the *Second Blast*. He was writing the *Appellation* and *Letter* more or less at the same time as the *First Blast* was published, and so he had no idea of the disastrous reception it would receive. The *Second Blast* would have been far more radical than the first, laying aside the issue of women rulers and making the case for the overthrow of all idolatrous tyrants. His outline indicates that he would have done this along the following lines:

- Monarchs and all political rulers do not derive the legitimacy of their rule solely from their birth or any human structures, but from obedience to God.

- Idolatry is open disobedience to God. No idolater, and no one who seeks to uphold or compel idolatry, has any right to public office of any kind.

- No subject has the duty to obey an idolatrous political ruler.

- All subjects have the right to depose and punish an idolatrous ruler.

Though the *Second Blast* was never published, here we have a clear outline of the most revolutionary stance that could be taken in Knox's time. Since it was appended to the *Appellation* and *Letter to the Commonality* and was therefore intended to be read together with them, we can assume that we are to interpret the *Appellation* and the *Letter* along this kind of trajectory. As we resume the story of Knox's life, we are about to see Knox and the leaders of the uprising against Mary of Guise put some of these ideas into practice.

CHAPTER FOUR

Returning to a Revolution

With the aftershocks of his *First Blast* still reverberating and in the aftermath of his *Appellation to the Nobility* and *Letter to the Commonality* in Scotland, Knox once again received letters urging him to return to his native land. It was now November 1558, his wife had recently given birth to their second son, and Knox was none too impressed with the summons. The last time he had received letters such as this, when his wife had just given birth to their first son, he had made his way to Dieppe to set sail for Scotland, only to discover that those intending to lead an uprising had acquired a severe case of cold feet. Now, however, there were indications that the persecution of Protestants would begin in earnest, and in response some Protestant lords in Angus and Fife and most of the commonality of Dundee had already met to sign a covenant to protect a preacher who had been summoned before the Privy Council for heresy. These lords were the men who wrote to Knox, and they also wrote to Calvin for good measure, knowing that he already had a track record in persuading Knox to undertake what he might otherwise have been reluctant to do. The situation that they described must have sounded familiar to Knox, since this was nothing less than what he himself had set forth as the litmus test of covenant faithfulness for both a ruler and the people in his *Appellation to the Nobility* and *Letter to the Commonality.* Would Protestant preaching be permitted by the former, and if not, would it be defended to the uttermost by the latter?

The men who urged him to return were also some of the prominent figures whom he had met and with whom he had stayed while on his preaching tour of 1555–56. The hope they expressed in their letter was still to persuade the Regent Mary of Guise to convert to, or at least to tolerate, Protestantism. Knox rightly thought the chances of either of these happening were slim. He set off for Scotland once again to be part of whatever the future would hold for Protestantism in his native land at what he realized was likely to be a critical moment.

He left in early 1559, intending to visit England first, but the *First Blast* continued to work against him. He sought safe conduct from Queen Elizabeth to travel to Scotland by land through England. He was refused. He asked again, thinking there must have been a mistake. She refused again. As he wrote ruefully to Anne Lock, "my *First Blast* hath blown from me all my friends in England."[1] Knox wrote a letter of protest to Sir William Cecil, Elizabeth's Secretary of State, first none-too-tactfully reminding him that he deserved the fires of hell for not speaking out against the persecution of Protestants during Mary's reign and then demanding a third time to be given safe passage through England. Not surprisingly, he did not receive a reply, so he set sail straight for Scotland instead.[2]

He arrived on May 2, 1559. That very day, unaware of who had just landed, Mary of Guise insisted that all preachers had to appear before her at Stirling on May 10. Messages were sent to her, pleading with her not to interfere with the preachers exercising their ministry. Her response was to threaten them with banishment. Protestants leaders were gathering supporters at Dundee, having decided that it would be a good idea to accompany their preachers to Stirling, and Knox immediately went to join them. On their way to Stirling, they stopped at Perth where more people joined them. They sent a message to the regent to say that

despite appearances, they weren't gathering an army, honestly; they were merely assembling as a peaceable crowd to show support for their pastors.

The regent cancelled the Stirling summons.

Some very relieved preachers went back to their homes.

The regent then reissued her summons for them to appear before her on the tenth, now with insufficient time for any of them to get there, and promptly outlawed them all in their absence.

Riot and Rebellion

The gloves were off, and the first armed confrontation can be traced to a sermon from Knox. On May 11 he preached in St. John's Kirk, the Perth parish church, as he had done regularly while staying there. After Mary of Guise's duplicity, he preached what was even by his own admission a particularly fiery sermon against idolatry. Not long after he had finished, the local Roman Catholic priest went to the church to say Mass. Some people from Knox's congregation were still there, and a boy told the priest exactly what he thought of the Mass in very Knoxian language. The priest threw a punch at the boy. The boy threw a stone at the priest. He missed, damaging one of the many statues of saints inside the church. Within minutes there was a full-scale, iconoclastic riot going on as the other people inside began smashing all the statues, breaking down the altars, and destroying the images. It wasn't long before people outside the church realized something was afoot inside and came to see what was going on. By this time there were no more idolatrous statues in St John's left to destroy, so a large crowd marched on several friaries in the city and ransacked them as well, destroying all the statues they could find and stealing the very good food and bedlinen they found there as well, for good measure.

When she heard about the rioting in Perth, the enraged regent put some troops together, many of them French, and decided to go in person to attack the Protestants in the city. She rapidly realized that she was completely outnumbered. There were approximately three thousand Protestants waiting for her, with reinforcements already on the way. Since she was the one who had marched on Perth, the Protestants maintained that theirs was a defensive and not an aggressive action, and all they wanted was the protection of their pastors and persecuted Protestants, and the right to practice their faith. An uneasy truce prevailed.

The Lords of the Congregation, as the Protestant leaders were called, met the following month in St Andrews, where Knox joined them, preaching in coastal towns on the way and leaving a trail of iconoclasm in his wake. As he approached St Andrews he heard that the Archbishop there had threatened to have him shot on sight if he dared to preach. On his first Sunday in the city he went straight into the pulpit of the parish church. Probably the most famous depiction of a scene

from Knox's life is the nineteenth-century Scottish artist Sir David Wilkie's painting, *The Preaching of John Knox before the Lords of Congregation*. Needless to say, no shots were fired, and with this, Knox also fulfilled the hope he had expressed all the way back in 1548, when he was a seriously ill galley slave on the French ship in the Tay Estuary. If you remember, he hoped that he would not die before he had preached again in the place where God had first called him to be a Protestant prophet.

Meanwhile, the supporters of the Lords of the Congregation continued to outnumber the regent's army, and she continued to refuse to allow freedom of worship to Protestants. Both sides avoided pitched battles, but the Lords of the Congregation took the city of Stirling before reaching Edinburgh, the seat of government, in June 1559, with yet more iconoclasm and rioting. The regent, who had fled to Dunbar, ordered them to leave the city. They refused, and Knox was elected as the minister of St. Giles, the largest and most important church in the capital.

A further uneasy truce was struck in which the regent permitted freedom of worship in Edinburgh (Protestants could worship at St. Giles and Mass would be said down the road in the chapel at the royal palace of Holyrood). No one was fooled, though. Mary was appealing to Henri II of France for help, and the Lords of the Congregation were trying to negotiate assistance from Elizabeth of England. Elizabeth was decidedly wary, however, about openly supporting a group of rebellious subjects against a lawful ruler, Roman Catholic or not. It didn't help that Knox was at the heart of the negotiations. Among other things, he reminded Elizabeth in his letters of her culpability in attending Mass during Mary's reign, and he reiterated that her legitimacy as a monarch depended on the fact that God had raised her up as his instrument and not upon her birth. It is doubtful

whether Sir William Cecil let her set eyes on any of Knox's letters. Knox even went to England, intending to conduct negotiations in person, but it would seem that Knox (and others, no doubt) recognized his limitations as a diplomat. The visit was cut short before Knox even met Cecil, and Knox returned to Scotland and settled in St Andrews, where his wife, children, and mother-in-law (now a widow) joined him.

That must have been quite a trek in its own right—Marjorie and her mother, Elizabeth, setting off from Geneva to Dieppe, Dieppe to London, and then London up to St Andrews with two-year-old Nathaniel and not-quite-one-year-old Eleazer in tow. Queen Elizabeth had enough sympathy to grant them safe conduct, even though she had earlier refused this three times for Knox. Surrounded by his family once again, Knox preached and pastored and set about writing *The History of the Reformation in Scotland* (key texts 8).

Some Significant Deaths . . .

By this time, Henri II of France had died. His son was now King François II, and his young wife, Mary, was therefore Queen Consort of France as well as Queen of Scotland. The implications of the new situation in France sharpened English thinking markedly. French help for the regent in Scotland was now much more likely to be forthcoming, and any such help would potentially be very threatening to England. The Lords of the Congregation realized this as well, and when they met in October 1559, they took the decision to depose the regent. As a result, the country was now ruled by the Protestant Lords of the Congregation. By November, though, they were quarreling among themselves, their army was drifting away, and Mary of Guise retook Edinburgh. A fiercely bracing sermon from Knox helped to reinvigorate the Lords and their army, but by this time Knox was somewhat on the margins. He returned to St Andrews rather than taking a role in the ongoing political negotiations. The success of a Protestant settlement was finally assured when, in January 1560, a fleet of English ships arrived and the following month the Treaty of Berwick was signed between Elizabeth and the Lords of the Congregation, which was intended to defend Scotland against French control.

The regent died in June after a long struggle with various illnesses, and in July a truce was signed. Parliament then met and established a Protestant settlement for the nation, abolishing papal authority, forbidding the Mass, and adopting a Protestant confession of faith. This made Scotland a covenant nation in Knox's eyes as he considered England had been since the Protestant legislation in the reign of Edward VI. Knox returned to Edinburgh, restored to his position as minister at St. Giles. It is always one thing to dismantle an old order, and quite another to create a new one. Knox was at the heart of building up as well as tearing down, involved in writing all the key documents that would shape the establishment of Protestantism in Scotland: *The Book of Common Order* (the new service book); *The Book of Discipline*, which set out the structure and organization of the new Protestant church; and the Protestant confession of faith, *The Scots Confession*. We will take a closer look at all three of them in key texts 6 and 7.

Two more deaths in late 1560, though, made the year even more profoundly significant for Knox. At a personal level, his wife, Marjorie, died at the age of about twenty-four. We do not know how she died, but it seems that in her last hours she was able to give a blessing to her two sons and to pray that they would be true worshipers of God and remain so all their lives. The death of Marjorie is one of the few purely personal matters that Knox mentions in *The History of the Reformation in Scotland*, where he speaks of the comfort given to him in a conversation with two noblemen

because of his grief for the death of his "dear bedfellow, Marjorie Bowes."[3] It was also at about the same time that the young French King François II died, leaving Mary a widow, who was free to return to her Scottish kingdom.

Key Texts 6

The Book of Common Order and *The Book of Discipline*

When we turn to the founding documents for the Protestant Reformation in Scotland we are also turning aside from works directly and entirely written by Knox. *The Book of Common Order, The Book of Discipline,* and *The Scots Confession* (key texts 7) are collaborative products, and it is impossible to be certain who wrote which sections. Also, as with all committee documents, we need to be wary about suggesting either that Knox will have been the source of any particular ideas or themes or even that he unequivocally

supported every aspect of what is contained in them. Nevertheless, in these central documents for the newly founded Protestant Kirk (Church) in Scotland, we see several important themes that we can trace in Knox's own work, and we also see the outcome of the movement in which Knox played such a significant role.

Each of these documents addresses a vital element needed for the building up of the new, national, Protestant church: liturgy, polity, and doctrine. That is to say the shape of worship, the structure of the church, and the core beliefs. *The Book of Common Order, The Book of Discipline,* and *The Scots Confession* tackled each of these respectively.

The Book of Common Order

The Book of Common Order, adopted for use in 1562, gives new shape to the worship of the nation by outlining the structure and content of services. It does not provide a set liturgy—fixed liturgical words and prayers—but rather, following Calvin's Genevan Prayer Book, it offers ministers a framework for services with each element in its proper order, but flexibility as to the precise content of what the minister will say. In fact, with only a few minor alterations, *The Book of Common Order* for the new Kirk was none other than the *Forme of Prayers* developed for use in the Genevan church for English exiles to whom Knox ministered, and this *Forme of Prayers* was in turn based heavily on Calvin's Prayer Book. We can therefore comfortably assume that *The Book of Common Order* resonates strongly in style and content with Knox's preferred approach to worship.

The structure is simple and centered around preaching. So, worship begins with a prayer of confession, followed by everyone singing a psalm, and then the minister prays for the assistance of the Holy Spirit before he begins his sermon.

Following the sermon are prayers of intercession for the church and the government, the singing of another psalm, and a blessing. When the Lord's Supper is to be celebrated, it is to be done seated around a table, just as was Knox's practice in Northumberland and as was one of his major points of resistance to the 1552 *Book of Common Prayer*.

At the end of the order of service, there is a brief explanation as to why the celebration of the Supper takes the form that it does: to make clear the rejection of the theology and practice of the Roman Catholic Mass and to follow the form of administration of the sacrament most closely aligned with the account of the Last Supper in order that, in a nutshell statement of Knox's own guiding principle in matters of worship, there is nothing done in the celebration of the sacrament that does not have warrant in God's Word.

In addition to the framework for regular services and services when the Lord's Supper is to be celebrated, there is also an outline for the celebration of the sacrament of baptism and a form for marriage. For all these there are sample prayers that ministers may use, but the encouragement is to see these prayers as models rather than set forms. As well, *The Book of Common Order* seeks to shape private piety by offering forms of prayer to be used by households in the morning and evening and suggested prayers before and after meals and on other occasions. Between weekly public worship and daily private devotions, *The Book of Common Order* sought to totally replace the Roman Catholic forms of piety that had shaped people's lives with a Protestant one, recognizing that a holistic approach was necessary for any attempt at the conversion of the nation.

The Book of Discipline

If *The Book of Common Order* focuses mainly on the worship of the new Protestant church, *The Book of Discipline* is in effect a manual for the structure and running of the church and for the role of the church in society. It, along with *The Scots Confession*, was drafted by six Johns, all of whom were ministers: John Knox, John Spottiswoode, John Willock, John Winram, John Row, and John Douglas. Never formally adopted by the Scottish Parliament, it nevertheless gives us an insight into the ideals and priorities of the leaders of the Reformation in Scotland, not just for the church but for the transformation of society.

The Book of Discipline adopts the continental Reformed model of ministers, elders, and deacons as the fundamental structure of the church, with ministers responsible for preaching, administering the sacraments, pastoral care, and discipline. The elders share with the minister the exercise of discipline. The deacons are responsible for the finances of the church and the care of the poor in the local parish. *The Book of Discipline* sets out the process by which each congregation is to choose its own minister and to elect elders and deacons from among its members. *The Book of Discipline* also proposes replacing the Roman Catholic bishops with "superintendents." Ten or twelve gifted ministers were to be chosen and appointed to designated areas as those most capable of planting churches and preaching during the transition period in which the number of competent Protestant ministers was not sufficient to fill all the parish vacancies. The superintendents were also to exercise oversight over the ministers within their area and to ensure that provision was being made for care of the poor and the education of children.

The Scottish Reformers, like the Lutheran and Reformed churches in Europe, longed for the formation of a godly society, established and maintained by the church and civil

authorities working together. The Scottish Reformers give considerable emphasis to the concept of church discipline—the church's right and responsibility to punish the unrepentant within the congregation who have committed certain offences. As we will see when we turn to *The Scots Confession*, the prominence accorded to church discipline is such that it becomes a third mark of the church—the third sign, alongside preaching and administering the sacraments, that denotes the true church. *The Book of Discipline* sets out the kinds of offenses to be regulated by the state (including blasphemy, adultery, murder, and perjury) and those to be dealt with by the church (such misdemeanors as drunkenness, inappropriate clothing or language, lewdness, but also unethical business practices and oppressing the poor).

With Matthew 18:15–18 as its guide, *The Book of Discipline* sets out a series of steps in a process of church discipline that culminates in excommunication: that is, offenders are barred from receiving the Lord's Supper until they publicly repent and are brought back into full communion with the church. Until that time, offenders also suffer the social alienation that goes with exclusion from the church community. Until those under the sanction of excommunication give evidence of repentance, no one is permitted to speak to them or conduct business with them other than their immediate family and those appointed by the church to have oversight over them. And at least in theory, no one was exempt from the church's disciplinary process, from the ministers themselves to the poorest member of the church to the monarch, and the aim was not merely punitive but restorative.

The Book of Discipline holds out a vision for the whole of society that does not just involve negative sanctions against transgressors but also seeks positive transformation, particularly in the realms of care for the poor and education. The ideal is that each church congregation is to provide for the

poor within its parish, such that all able-bodied people would be able to find work, and the church would provide for the needy. Most particularly, the ideals expressed in *The Book of Discipline* had a lasting impact in the area of education reform. At the time, Scotland was considered to be one of the more educationally backward nations in Europe. If the proposals in *The Book of Discipline* had been adopted, it would have become the first European nation to introduce compulsory universal basic education. The visionary intent was to ensure that all children, regardless of economic status, be given sufficient education to be able to read, to learn the catechism, and to understand the basics of Latin. Financial help would be provided for those parents unable to afford to sustain their children in schooling, and any children who showed particular aptitude would be encouraged to continue. Those considered to have reached the limits of their intellectual abilities would be taught a trade or a craft.

The money that should have been devoted to make this vision a reality was siphoned off. The intention had been to fund it from the revenues of the now-closed Roman Catholic abbeys and other sources taken over from the Roman Catholic Church, but the Scottish nobility rapidly took charge of these sources of income for themselves. Even so, the ideal held out by *The Book of Discipline* continued to inspire efforts toward a renewal of education, and one facet of it in particular has drawn attention. *The Book of Discipline* refers simply to "children" and "youth," so it is not clear whether girls were included in this compulsory education program. Since they are not excluded and since it was slowly becoming more commonplace in England that girls should be given some schooling, we can perhaps assume that girls were included in the provisions laid out for the reform of education in Scotland too, at least up to the most

basic level. Both of Knox's wives were well-enough educated to help him in his work (we've already met his first wife, Marjorie; we'll meet his second wife, Margaret, shortly). As we'll see in the final chapter, his friend and correspondent, Anne Lock, was a poet and translator of Calvin. Knox himself clearly respected educated women, and therefore presumably valued education for women.

Key Texts 7

The Scots Confession

Like *The Book of Discipline*, *The Scots Confession* was commissioned from the six ministerial Johns, and we are told that they managed to write it in four days. It was duly ratified by Parliament, becoming the official statement of faith for the new Protestant Kirk until it was replaced by the Westminster Confession in 1647.

The Scots Confession begins with a preface that is notable for urging readers to get in touch with the authors if they think they find anything in it that is contrary to Scripture:

> If any man will note in this our Confession any article or sentence repugning to God's holy word, that it would please him . . . for Christian charity's sake, to admonish us of the same in [writing]; and we of our honour and fidelity do promise unto him satisfaction from [scripture] or else reformation of that which he shall prove to be amiss.

Here is one of the clearest possible statements of the Reformation principle that all doctrinal formulations are subordinate to and must be based on Scripture. The theme is resumed more formally in chapters 18–20 of the confession itself, which articulate the standard position that while the

councils of the church might well produce valuable statements on matters of doctrine, their worth is to be assessed only on the basis of how well they accord with Scripture.

The Scots Confession consist of twenty-five "chapters" (each chapter is only a paragraph or so in length), treating the nature of God (chapter 1); the creation of human beings and sin (chapters 2 and 3); God's saving promises and providential care for his people, shown in the narrative of his dealings with Israel (chapters 4 and 5); the person and work of Christ (chapters 6–11); the Holy Spirit (chapter 12); the relationship between faith, works, and the law (chapters 13–15); issues to do with the nature of the church, the subordination of the church to Scripture, the sacraments, and the relationship between the church and the government (chapters 16 and 18–24); the intermediate state of the saved and the lost, awaiting the final judgment (chapter 17); and a final chapter (25) on the general resurrection, judgment, and the life to come.

Obviously, it is not possible to separate John Knox's contribution to the confession from that of his colleagues or to state that every aspect of the confession is a precise expression of Knox's own views. We can simply say that what is found in the confession is upheld by Knox as a core statement of belief for the new Protestant church in Scotland. It is also true that there isn't much that is distinctive in the confession. It is a brief compendium of central ideas for Reformed Protestantism, and there are echoes of many sources. This includes apparently taking its ringing opening statement about total commitment to God—"We confess and acknowledge one God alone, to whom alone we must cleave, whom alone we must serve, whom alone we must worship, in whom alone we put our trust"—pretty much straight from the confession to which the students at the Genevan Academy were required to subscribe.

All we will do here is highlight some themes and emphases that have attracted attention, and also some aspects of the confession that resonate with important elements in Knox's own theology. So, for example, we have seen how significant the Old Testament is for Knox in terms of his own self-understanding and also in the direct correlations that he discerns between God's dealings with Israel and his involvement in contemporary events. With chapters 4 and 5 of the confession given over to a brief retelling of the Old Testament narrative in the light of the promise of a Redeemer, *The Scots Confession* in fact gives more attention to the Old Testament and the significance of God's people Israel than any of the more famous confessions and catechisms of the period.

Perhaps the most interesting and suggestive section of all in *The Scots Confession*, though, is chapter 8 on the doctrine of election. For the distinctiveness of the treatment of the subject here, it helps to give an outline of Knox's position as he expresses it in his only major treatise on a single doctrine, his *An Answer to a Great Number of Blasphemous Cavillations Written by an Anabaptist and Adversary to God's Eternal Predestination*. This lengthy document was written in 1559, a year before *The Scots Confession*. It is not a systematic presentation of Knox's views as such, but a paragraph-by-paragraph refutation of an anonymous work on the subject. As he asserts, he follows Calvin (and also Beza) closely in terms of his overall position on the doctrine.[4] This means Knox's emphasis falls on the inability of human beings to turn to God unaided, such that salvation is all of grace. Only as God gives the gift of faith to those chosen from all eternity are they enabled to turn to God. Those whom God has elected to save demonstrate his mercy, and the reprobate demonstrate God's judgment.

While all hear the general call of the gospel, the Holy Spirit enables the eternally elect to respond in faith. This is God's effectual call (or what Knox calls a "vocation of purpose"), which will issue both in their justification through the gift of faith and their sanctification as they bear the fruits of their election in good works. Therefore, both faith and good works stem from God's election, rather than in any way being the cause of God's election. Moreover there is no sense in which this effectual calling is understood as the violation of the will. Rather if we are left to ourselves, because we are alienated from God, we freely choose to turn away from God. By the work of the Holy Spirit, our wills are in fact set free for God, and we freely turn toward God. Where Knox departs from Calvin and Beza—or rather, where he is less certain than they—is in his ambivalence over the question of full double-predestination.

Calvin and Beza maintain that it is equally God's active choice to reject some (by choosing not to give them the gift of faith) as to save others. At times, Knox appears to agree with this position, but more often he implies that while God actively chooses to save some, he simply passes over the rest.

Knox's treatise offers a thoroughly conventional account of the subject from a Reformed perspective, and a summary of these sorts of points might well be what we would expect of a chapter on election in *The Scots Confession*. In fact, we get nothing of the sort. This chapter has very little indeed to say about God's eternal choosing of individuals for salvation—it simply states, following Ephesians 1, that the elect are chosen by grace alone in Christ before the foundation of the world. It also has almost nothing at all to say about the rejected (or the reprobate), except to mention in passing that they exist. Instead, the focus of this chapter on election is almost exclusively on Jesus Christ—fully divine, fully human—as the appointed Mediator and Redeemer through whom victory over sin and death and our reconciliation with the Father have been won.

From the way that *The Scots Confession* as a whole describes the relationship between God and human beings it clearly belongs within the same basic Reformed framework as Knox set out in his treatise. That is to say, according to the eternal predestination of God there are the elect to whom the gift of faith will be given and for whom the sacraments and all the promises of God will be effectual; and there are the rejected, who will not receive the gift of faith and so who will be condemned, as those to whom the work of Christ does not apply. The confession as a whole does not indicate a major shift in thinking on the doctrine. Even so, the chapter on election itself stands out, and there is nothing in Knox's own thoroughly conventional Reformed treatment of the doctrine to hint at the christological focus found there. It is not surprising that Karl Barth, the twentieth-century Reformed theologian who developed his own highly distinctive "christological" approach to election, took some inspiration from the way in which *The Scots Confession* associates the doctrine so strongly with the person and work of Christ.

Turning to the understanding of the church found in the confession, as you have seen in the key texts section on *The Book of Discipline*, the Scottish church makes discipline the third "mark" of the church. This is formally stated in chapter 18 and means that in terms of the wider Reformed family at the time, Scotland follows Martin Bucer rather than

John Calvin in asserting that there are three marks (or signs) of the true church rather than two. For Calvin, the church exists wherever the Word is truly preached and the sacraments of baptism and the Lord's Supper are duly administered. For *The Scots Confession*, the third mark of the church is the right and obligation of the church to impose sanctions on its members for behavior deemed to be inappropriate, so that "vice is repressed and virtue nourished." We saw some of the ways in which that operated in practice in *The Book of Discipline*. Church discipline is a concept that had long been important to Knox. He had criticized the English church before the Privy Council in 1553 for the lack of a formal disciplinary structure, and the confession of faith held by the English congregation at Geneva, of which Knox was a pastor, maintained the three marks of the true church rather than Calvin's two.

Finally, with regard to the sacraments, while there is nothing unique or distinctive in what *The Scots Confession* has to say, either about baptism or the Lord's Supper (the only two sacraments recognized as having scriptural warrant by Protestants), there is a strong connection between Knox's own understanding of the sacraments in general and the Lord's Supper in particular, and what is presented in the confession. We know this because we have various statements of Knox's views in his other writings. In particular, of course, there is his condemnation of the Roman Catholic Mass throughout his life, and it is no surprise to see a vigorous rejection of the Mass in the confession, as well as in *The Book of Common Order*. In addition, though, Knox wrote a short tract setting out his positive view of the Lord's Supper in the early 1550s. In this he strongly asserts that the heart of the Supper is the way in which the Holy Spirit unites us to Christ, not by any transforming work in the elements of bread and wine, but in lifting us up to Christ in a spiritual feeding upon his body and blood. That spiritual feeding on Christ, through union with him in his ascended humanity by the Spirit, is held out for us as we eat and drink the bread and wine. The physical act helps us to grasp the mystery of the spiritual reality to which it points. The Lord's Supper therefore nourishes us spiritually and helps us to grow in grace, individually and together. This is because it is both the sacrament of our personal union with Christ by the Spirit and of our union with one another in the church, the body of Christ, by the Spirit.

Anyone who knows what Calvin has to say about the Lord's Supper will recognize strong similarities between Knox's understanding and Calvin's, and we also find a

summary of just such a position in *The Scots Confession*. The Lord's Supper and baptism are the gracious gift of God to us to strengthen our faith, to apply to our hearts the promises of God, and to hold out to us the reality of our union with Christ. *The Scots Confession* therefore affirms very strongly that the sacraments are both a sign and a seal of God's promises and of our union with Christ. The confession is as vigorous in rejecting the idea that the sacraments are merely symbolic as it is in rejecting aspects of the Roman Catholic understanding of the Mass. So, the writers of the confession state that "we utterly condemn the vanity of those who affirm the sacraments to be nothing else than naked and bare signs" and "if anyone slanders us by saying that we affirm . . . the sacraments to be symbols and nothing more, they are libelous." Rather, the sacraments do indeed convey the reality of what they promise to us when they are received in faith. So, in baptism, "we are engrafted into Christ Jesus" and in the Lord's Supper "Christ Jesus is so joined with us that He becomes very nourishment and food of our souls," not through the transubstantiation of the elements, but through the work of the Holy Spirit in those who receive in faith, who lifts us to Christ and so unites us to him that we feed upon Christ's body and blood.[5] These sorts of statements not only situate *The Scots Confession* within the overall Protestant rejection of the Roman Catholic understanding of the Mass but also locate it within the passionate intra-Protestant disputes about the nature of the Lord's Supper. In these disputes Lutherans were ranged against the Reformed, and the Reformed, such as those coming from a Zwinglian perspective and Calvin, fought about it among themselves as well. It is the Zwinglian stream of thinking in particular that is being attacked in *The Scots Confession*'s statements that criticize a view of the

sacraments as "naked signs," and its positive statements place it within the stream of thinking associated with Calvin and Bucer.

With these three texts—*The Scots Confession*, *The Book of Common Order*, and *The Book of Discipline*—the foundations of the Protestant settlement are in place. We now pick up the life of Knox with his dramatic final years, as the Roman Catholic Mary, Queen of Scots, arrives to take the helm of her officially Protestant nation.

CHAPTER FIVE

A Roman Catholic Queen and a Protestant Realm

At first it wasn't clear whether Mary would come to Scotland to assume personal rule or would remain in France. In early 1561 the Scottish Parliament sent a delegation to France to ask Mary to return. A condition of her coming back to her now Protestant realm was supposed to be that Mass would not be said in public or in private. The negotiator backed down on this almost immediately, as long as she promised to recognize the Protestant church, which she said that she would do. Mary landed in August 1561, and on her first Sunday, Mass was said at the Chapel Royal at Holyrood, amid noisy protests outside. Knox was predictably furious, and that Sunday in St. Giles he spoke out against the Queen in his sermon. The following Sunday he preached even more passionately against the Mass.

Even so, Sir Nicholas Throckmorton, whom Elizabeth I of England had asked to keep an eye on the situation in Scotland, commented that almost everyone seemed to be favorably impressed by the Queen "saving John Knox, that thundereth out of the pulpit" and who was, he feared, likely to ruin everything.[1] Many thought that at the very least Mary might be persuaded to tolerate Protestantism, and perhaps even to convert. Knox was convinced from the outset that she was not to be trusted, and as we have seen all along, his favored style with monarchs was always to harangue rather than seek to persuade.

About a month after she arrived there was the first of four confrontational meetings between Mary and Knox, as recorded by Knox in *The History of the Reformation in Scotland*. Mary had read the *First Blast*, and in fact she had initially indicated that she would not set foot in Scotland until Knox was banished from it. She had been persuaded to return anyway, but at this first stormy meeting she immediately raised the *First Blast* and its threat to her authority. Knox remarked that he had written it specifically against Mary Tudor in England and maintained that provided she did not persecute Protestants he would accept her rule—in the same way that Paul had been obliged to accept Nero's! Mary pressed him further, challenging Knox's right to teach that the people could maintain a religion contrary to that of their rulers and to teach that they had the right to take up arms against their rulers. Good Christian subjects surely ought to follow the God-given command to obey their princes. Knox retorted with a summary of the theology of rebellion that we outlined in key texts 4 and 5: that all subjects have the right to oppose a prince who commits idolatry and persecutes the godly.[2]

Mary summoned Knox to a second meeting after Knox had preached against her love of dancing and on the ignorance and vanity of monarchs in general. And then she called a third meeting after some Protestant Lords had arrested a priest for saying Mass. The arrest was in accordance with laws passed by Parliament, so Knox defended their actions and demanded she should do likewise. In fact, Mary had not yet ratified any legislation passed by the Parliament before she arrived, and the subject was discreetly avoided when her first Parliament met, to Knox's fury. At any rate, the official meeting ended in stalemate, but the following day they met more informally. This was perhaps the most conciliatory conversation they ever had. In this meeting, among other things, Mary gave Knox what turned

out to be wise counsel concerning an upcoming election for a church position and asked his advice about a prominent nobleman's failing marriage.[3]

Then rumors began to spread that Mary was seeking marriage with Don Carlos, the son of Philip II of Spain. Knox preached with all his usual bluntness and vehemence against any prospect of her marriage to a papist, warning that this would bring down God's vengeance against Scotland. In this, he succeeded in offending many Protestants as well as Roman Catholics and infuriated the Queen so much that she burst into tears of anger and frustration when, at her summons, they had a fourth and final official meeting.[4]

These four meetings between Knox and the Queen were relatively private, with a handful of courtiers in attendance. The next time that Knox and the Queen met it would once again be at her summons, but this time he would be on trial before her and the Privy Council. In 1563, the Queen chose to spend time in Stirling, and some members of her court who had stayed behind in Edinburgh went to celebrate Mass at Holyrood Chapel. A Protestant mob burst in and threatened the priest, and the Protestant authorities prosecuted twenty-two people for attending (as in fact was required by the law passed by Parliament, although still not ratified by the Queen). Two of the leaders of the mob were arrested and due to be tried, so Knox sent urgent letters asking Protestants to hasten to Edinburgh to support them. The trial was abandoned. At the hearing before her and the Privy Council, the Queen sought to have Knox's letters interpreted as an attempt to raise a rebellion against her, and so as an act of treason. This was firmly rejected by the Privy Council. It was, after all, a little awkward to indict Knox for treason when he was encouraging people to show their support for the law of the land.[5]

Though this was the final time that Mary and Knox would encounter one another face-to-face, it was not the final time that Knox managed to infuriate her. Of course, his preaching continued to do that on a regular basis, and during the General Assembly of the Church of Scotland in 1564, Knox reiterated the right of subjects to take up arms against ungodly rulers as the instruments of God's vengeance upon them.[6] As we will see, not many years later, as Mary's life and reign disintegrated into chaos, Knox would openly advocate her execution.

Interesting Marriages

For the moment, though, we are still in 1564, and that year even his private life managed to enrage the Queen. On March 25, to universal astonishment, the fifty-year-old

Knox married the seventeen-year-old Margaret Stewart, a daughter of an old friend of his, Lord Ochiltree. While the age difference between them caused something of a scandal, Mary was furious to the point of threatening to banish him into exile because Knox had dared to marry a member of the royal house of Stewart. These were empty threats, but vicious propaganda against the marriage circulated for some time. In all likelihood it was a marriage of convenience, but it certainly seemed happy and successful enough. Like his first wife, Margaret was an educated woman who helped him with his work, and by all accounts John and Margaret also had a vibrant social life, frequently entertaining major Protestant figures to lively and enjoyable supper parties. They had three daughters, Martha, Margaret, and Elizabeth, and we are told that although it went against the usual custom Knox chose the name Margaret for his second daughter as a tribute to his wife.[7]

For some years now, however, although a minister at St. Giles with strong popular support, Knox had been on the outside of political life. He had little direct influence and was seen as something of an embarrassment. From the moment that Mary arrived, Knox had been seen as a serious liability by many Protestant leaders as they attempted the delicate maneuverings needed to reach tolerable compromises with the new Queen. Knox undoubtedly felt grimly vindicated in his suspicions of her from the outset as she showed herself to be seemingly at once unstable and bent on self-destruction in the tumultuous final year or so of her reign. In 1565, to the wrath of many of the Protestant Lords, she married her cousin, Lord Henry Stewart Darnley, who had dynastic links to the English throne. This led to a brief uprising against her. It failed, and the leaders had to flee to England, under condemnation of treason. It hadn't taken long for Mary to work out that she had probably made a mistake in her choice of husband, though, and she refused to grant Darnley the crown matrimonial—that is, the right to reign in her place if she died. Exploiting this, and in response to the threat of death (and the forfeiture of their estates) for the leaders of the attempted uprising, a very convoluted plot was hatched. Darnley and others would murder David Riccio, the Queen's secretary and possible lover and the one whom Darnley had come to believe was largely responsible for Mary's unwillingness to give him the crown matrimonial. In return for getting off scot free for the murder and for their support in getting him the crown rights he sought, Darnley promised he would pardon all the Lords involved in the uprising. Knox almost certainly knew about the plot, since every single one of his friends did—and so, it seems, did just about everyone else except Mary and Riccio themselves.

Darnley and a group of other men burst in on Mary one evening in March 1566, while she was having a supper party with several friends. Riccio was there too. She was six months pregnant with the future James VI of Scotland and I of England. One of the men put a pistol to her stomach

while the others seized Riccio, stabbed him in front of her, dragged him out, and continued stabbing him to death in the adjoining room. At this point, Darnley more or less took Mary hostage and took it upon himself to dissolve Parliament. Mary was imprisoned in Stirling Castle but seemingly managed to persuade Darnley that his coconspirators intended to destroy him too, so he helped Mary to escape, and together they fled to Dunbar, where the Earl of Bothwell raised an army for her. At this point, all the Riccio conspirators and all the prominent people who had known about the conspiracy fled. That included Knox, who skulked in Ayrshire for a while before taking an extended holiday to the north of England to visit his sons, who were being educated there under the wing of the Bowes family.

Darnley tried to protest his innocence in the plot to kill Riccio, but Mary had seen a copy of the bond Darnley had signed, committing himself to the whole conspiracy. There are also some suggestions that Darnley may have tried to have Mary killed on various occasions in order to assume the throne himself. At any rate, the writing was on the wall for him, one way or another. So it was for Mary too, although she might not have thought so at the time. From this point on, her life and her reign rapidly spiraled completely out of control. The sequence of events in the next six months is quite dizzying. Here is just a summary of events in 1567:

> February: Darnley is mysteriously murdered. His residence exploded (someone ignited the gunpowder stored under the house), but he actually died of strangulation. Suspicion immediately fell on Lord Bothwell and also on Mary herself as being involved in his death, even if not the actual perpetrators. This can't be proven, as letters incriminating Mary were probably at least partly forged, and Bothwell was tried and acquitted.

April 19: Bothwell receives a petition from prominent lords and churchmen, effectively urging him to marry Mary.

April 24: Bothwell and a company of soldiers escort Mary to his home in Dunbar, purportedly for her own safety (it seems as though she went willingly, rather than this being, in effect, a kidnapping).

May 7: Bothwell divorces his wife, saying that he had committed adultery with one of her servants (the story of Bothwell's first marriage is a tale in itself, but we can't go into it here).

May 15: Bothwell and Mary are married at the Palace of Holyrood. Sir William Drury, a close observer of all events related to Mary on behalf of Queen Elizabeth, remarked in a letter to William Cecil that while all of this might have looked as though it were forced on Mary, it was known to be far otherwise.

June: Mary and Bothwell are faced with an army led by the Protestant Lords. She surrenders and is imprisoned in Lochleven Castle.

July: just after miscarrying twins, Mary signs a document abdicating in favor of her one-year-old son,
James. The Protestant James Stewart, Earl of Moray,
is appointed as regent. It is with this event that
Knox's *History of the Reformation in Scotland* (our
final key text) ends.

The Final Years

Knox returned to Scotland after his time in England in June
1566. Throughout all the twists and turns of 1567 he was
thundering against Mary from the pulpit at St. Giles and
calling openly for her execution. His preaching was so
inflammatory and violent that Queen Elizabeth's agent, Sir
Nicholas Throckmorton, visited Knox and tried to persuade
him to at least moderate his language a little. Not a chance.
To Knox, this entire series of events had proven him to be
correct in his suspicions of Mary all along. Not only had she
wrecked the stability of the country and its Protestant
settlement on her return by insisting on promoting Roman
Catholicism, she had also plunged the country into utter
chaos largely because of her folly and her sin since, as Knox
was convinced, she was an adulteress and murderer. There
was no way that he was going to hold back in the pulpit—
and he was preaching to large congregations as often as five
times a week.

Knox also preached at the opening of Parliament in
December 1567 while Mary was imprisoned at Lochleven
Castle. This was the Parliament that finally ratified the mea-
sures for reforming the church that were decided in 1560.
As well, the Parliament formally accepted Mary's abdication
and accused her of being implicated in the death of Darnley.
Not too long after that, Knox once again considered all his
public vehemence against Mary justified as she escaped

from her imprisonment, managed to raise another army, and marched against Regent Moray. Her forces were routed, and she fled to England to begin the long route to the scaffold there in 1587. You can't help but suspect that if he had lived long enough to see the trouble that Mary caused to Queen Elizabeth, Knox would have relished writing one of his scolding letters to her to say that if only she and others had listened to him and executed Mary earlier, it would have saved Elizabeth and many others nearly two decades of further trouble.

In the meanwhile, Regent Moray was assassinated early in 1570 and Scotland then descended into civil war between supporters of the deposed Queen Mary and the infant King. In the autumn of 1570, Knox had a stroke and lost his speech. His enemies gloated that God had struck him dumb as a punishment, but within a few weeks he was on his feet and preaching at St. Giles again. The vagaries of the civil war meant that Mary's forces took Edinburgh Castle, but Knox was predictably unstoppable, still preaching against Mary a little farther down the road at St. Giles and openly demanding her execution. Advocating the execution of a monarch, however, even a deposed one who had brought about a civil war, made him deeply unpopular with moderate Protestants as well as Roman Catholics, and his own life was now under threat. He was publicly accused of treason, and papers against him were nailed to the door of St. Giles. Some prominent former allies of Knox deserted to the Queen's side, and with her supporters in a position of strength, orders were issued on April 30, 1571, that all supporters of the King were to leave Edinburgh that very day. There was no more prominent enemy of the Queen in Edinburgh than John Knox. He refused point blank to go. A colleague came and urged him to leave because not only was his decision to stay risking the lives of his wife and daughters but also the lives of many of the local people who supported him and were preparing to prevent any attempt to seize or harm him. Eventually—but not until five days later—he was persuaded to take his wife and young family to safety.

They made their way slowly to St Andrews, and he remained there for the rest of the civil war. He preached as he was able, although his health was clearly failing. We have a moving account from the diary of James Melville—later a minister but then a fifteen-year-old student at the university—of how Knox would walk very slowly to the parish church, using a walking stick and supported by his secretary, Richard Bannatyne, and of how Bannatyne and others had to lift him into the pulpit. Melville heard him preach on the book of Daniel and said that at the start of his sermons, he would speak quietly as he analyzed the text, but that when he came to draw parallels between the text and the present situation

in Scotland, he was a man transformed. Melville says he found this side of Knox's preaching so compelling (and terrifying) that he could barely hold his pen to write, and that this feeble man became "as active and vigorus that he was lyk to ding the pulpit in blads and fly out of it."[8] You don't need to know sixteenth-century Scots to work out what he was saying there. To the end, then, Knox the Protestant prophet did as he had done from the very moment that he began his preaching ministry from that very same pulpit: drawing from the Old Testament prophets a passionate message of how he understood the will and the workings of God for his own time.

Knowing he could not have long to live, Knox made his will. He provided for his sons by his first marriage, and also his nephew, as well as his young wife and their daughters.

With Margaret's help he was also at work preparing one last pamphlet for publication: *An Answer to a Letter of a Jesuit named Tyrie*, first written six years earlier against Tyrie's defense of the Roman Catholic Church as the true church. As he was finishing the revisions he received news that Elizabeth Bowes had died. We will have more to say about Knox's relationship with Elizabeth and other important women in his more private life in the final chapter. For the moment, when the *Answer* was published, it came with an appendix, a copy of a letter he had written to Elizabeth in 1554, as an example of the kinds of spiritual troubles on which she had sought his advice and of the nature of his correspondence with her. At the close of both of their lives he wanted to put an end once and for all to the rumors about their relationship and to show that their long and close acquaintance had been centered on his pastoral concern and counsel for her troubled conscience and spiritual struggles.[9]

In July 1572, the civil war ended in a truce and some members of St. Giles invited him back. He and his family returned, and he preached at the end of August. But the voice that had been like a sounding trumpet was now so quiet that few could hear him. From this point on, a smaller space was found, and he preached as often as he was physically able to do so.

By November he was clearly fading fast, and in his final weeks a steady procession of friends and visitors sought him at his home. Having passed his final day in the company of a friend, and with his wife reading Scripture to him, praying with him and tending to him, John Knox died peacefully, late in the evening of November 24, 1572. His funeral took place at St. Giles two days later. As the Earl of Morton said of him in the eulogy, he neither feared nor flattered any flesh.

Key Texts 8

The History
of the Reformation in Scotland

Much of what we know about Knox, as well as the Scottish Reformation itself, comes from Knox's monumental *The History of the Reformation in Scotland*. It covers the years 1492 to 1567 in a series of five books, and it takes up nearly two volumes in the six-volume standard edition of his complete works. Knox was working on it over the last twelve years of his life, beginning in 1559, as events in Scotland reached a crisis point, and making his final changes to it in the year before his death. It is a massive undertaking, but it has proved to be difficult to categorize and to evaluate. How factually reliable is it? Is it more of a memoir than a history? Does Knox reframe events for theological or personal purposes? The scholarly consensus seems to be that

while it is fundamentally reliable, it is more of a theological interpretation of events than an account of history as we would generally understand that today. That is hardly surprising, given Knox's understanding of his calling, his passionate belief in God's providential involvement in the unfolding of all events and actions, and the fact that post-Enlightenment categories and presuppositions are never going to be entirely appropriate for pre-modern texts such as this one.

Writing history is, for Knox, essentially the task of uncovering God's story. That is, human history is the arena of God's action, in which his ultimate purposes are being worked out. *The History of the Reformation in Scotland* takes its place alongside works with a similar purpose, such as John Foxe's *Acts and Monuments*, first published in 1563 and better known as his *Book of Martyrs*. Foxe was one of Knox's supporters while he was ministering to the English congregation in Frankfurt, and in this book he attempts to give a history of the martyrs from the early church onward, focusing especially on England and giving detailed and harrowing accounts of the Protestants tried, tortured, and killed under Mary Tudor.

Like Foxe, Knox considers that the task of the chronicler of events is to seek to interpret what has happened from a "God's-eye" perspective. This means that Knox's *History of the Reformation in Scotland* is an extension of his role as both preacher and especially as prophet. The prophet is the one able to discern the hand and the will of God in events. This is the case retrospectively, and then with regard to the present, and also in anticipation of the future. Moreover, just as the preacher's task is to exhort the people to live according to the revealed will of God in Scripture, so Knox's *History* is intended to achieve similar aims for its readers. The *History* is written to strengthen those who have given themselves to the cause of the Reformation, to encourage the waverers to see that by allying themselves with the Protestant movement they are swimming with the stream of God's will for the nation of Scotland, and to warn those who oppose God's will in this regard of the dire personal and societal consequences, through the example of the times when the punishment of God has been manifest, in Scripture and in history, for defying his will.

This means that in the pages of the *History* we see all the chief characteristics that we have noted in Knox's writing from the very outset, in particular the paradigmatic significance of the Old Testament for the interpretation of past and present events. As in his earlier writing in relation to both England and Scotland, Knox makes direct equations between God's dealings with his people Israel and events in Scottish history right up into Knox's present. Individuals are cast in terms of the Old Testament figures to whom Knox thinks they correspond. More generally, though, the broad pattern of Israel's walk with God, as the chosen people who fall away from God and receive his punishment, but from among whom a remnant will remain faithful, is the overall lens through which he considers that the Scottish Reformation is to be understood. Needless to say, the embattled and persecuted resistors of the Roman Catholic Church down the ages are the faithful remnant. They are the "true church" in the midst of the idolatrous Roman Catholic "false church," and God is bringing about the vindication of that true remnant through the establishment of a Protestant settlement.

Another key theme that surfaces in *History*, as it does throughout Knox's works, is the idea that idolatry is the major touchstone for obedience to or defiance of God. As

before, idolatry is not simply understood as worship of false gods, but false worship of the one true God, either by directing any form of worship to another (Mary or the saints) or by rites and ceremonies that go beyond the manner of worship that he considers to be proscribed in the Scriptures. Idolatry (and resistance to it) is the preeminent indication for Knox of whether or not someone is adhering to the covenant that God has established. By committing idolatry a person and a nation will bring down the judgment of God and will abrogate a place within the covenant in which God will be their God and they his people. While God in his mercy will turn again to an individual or nation that repents of backsliding, nothing but punishment and rejection can be expected for a person or nation that persistently defies his commandments.

When we interpret *The History of the Reformation in Scotland*, we therefore have to recognize that while this is a new genre for Knox and while it is the most sustained work he ever wrote, Knox's intent in writing it is fundamentally the same as in his letters and his *First Blast* and indeed his preaching. There is profound continuity of purpose and style. The same concerns drive Knox here as have driven him since the outset of his public career, and there is integrity across the different genres that is rooted in his understanding of his calling as a preacher and a prophet.

CHAPTER SIX

More than Marys: The Other Women in Knox's Life

In our journey through Knox's life and work, several women have been mentioned a very great deal—mainly, it has to be said, Roman Catholic rulers by the name of Mary. There was Mary Tudor, Queen of England, who succeeded Edward VI; then Mary of Guise, the regent of Scotland, who was the mother of the last Mary to feature so prominently in Knox's life—Mary, Queen of Scots. But other women have quietly slipped into the narrative at various points as well. Marjorie, his first wife; his second wife, Margaret; and also his mother-in-law, Elizabeth Bowes, and his friend Anne Lock. This final chapter is dedicated to these important women in Knox's life and to how what we know of Knox's relationships with them ought to shape our understanding of him just as much as his more famous dealings with more famous women.

Knox's fiery outbursts against the Marys in person and in print are the very public side of his dealings with women, the side that the majority of people in his time and later have seen, and so they are the basis for the myth of his supposed and almost pathological misogynism. This is very far from the full picture. We are also talking about a husband whose wives, as we have seen, were full helpmates to him, educated and intelligent enough to be of great assistance in his work. We are also talking about a pastor who met with and wrote to various groups of women in England and Scotland concerning their spiritual troubles. And we are talking about a man who dealt with some far-from-easy relationships with women with delicacy, care, and respect. Knox sought and valued the help and advice he received from them, and their friendship clearly meant much to him.

Knox's Wives

Ironically, the women in his life about whom we know the least are his two wives. Even so, Knox and his first wife, Marjorie, seemed to have forged a strong relationship under complex circumstances. As we have seen in the account of his life, when Knox was finally able to marry her, in the teeth of major opposition from her father, his mother-in-law also left her husband to live with them in Geneva. Not surprisingly, this was the subject of lewd and scurrilous speculation, particularly in Roman Catholic pamphlets. Even so, the three of them braved the public mockery (and no doubt the behind-their-backs sniggering), and the attempts to pin scandal on the arrangement were almost certainly without foundation. Whatever the private tensions that might have arisen from having Marjorie's mother as part of their household, to their friends John and Marjorie seem to have been good company and a well-matched couple. An invitation to join the Knoxes appears to have been welcome—Marjorie's gifts as a hostess were recognized and admired, and we know that Marjorie was able to help Knox with his writing and his work.

As we have seen, his wife Marjorie's death in 1560 was one of the very few personal matters to be included in Knox's *History of the Reformation in Scotland*. It seems that Elizabeth, his now-widowed mother-in-law, returned to England after her daughter's death. But in 1562, Knox asked her to return to help to look after his two young sons, both still under ten years old, which she did. We've also seen that his remarriage in 1564 set tongues wagging on several fronts. First, he married someone with connections

to the Scottish royal family, but also because Margaret Stewart was seventeen and John Knox was fifty. Even at a time when a wide difference in age between husbands and wives was more common than it tends to be today, this was enough to occasion comment. Knox's relationships with women kept the sixteenth-century equivalent of the gossip columns spilling ink to the end. Once again, however, there is nothing to suggest that this marriage was anything but a happy one, and it seems that their friends greatly enjoyed spending time in their company. After the marriage Knox sent his sons, by now sixteen and seventeen years old, to continue their education under the watchful eye of their Bowes relatives in England, and it seems that Elizabeth went with them. As we saw in the previous chapter, when things in Scotland became rather too hot to handle—in the aftermath of the Riccio murder—Knox took a six-month holiday to visit them in 1566.

Elizabeth Bowes and Anne Lock

The two women who figure most prominently in Knox's correspondence, though, and so the ones about whose relationship to Knox we know the most, are his mother-in-law Elizabeth Bowes and his long-time friend, Anne Lock.[1] What has been preserved of the correspondence between them offers us the clearest insight into a very different Knox than the one who marches, fulminating, across the public stage. Of the fifty or so letters of Knox to survive, almost thirty are to Mrs. Bowes. None of her letters to Knox were preserved, but she treasured his letters all her life. They were returned to Knox when she died, and so became part of Knox's collected writings. Of the other surviving letters by Knox, thirteen are to Mrs. Lock. Whereas Knox is very much a spiritual counselor to Mrs.

Bowes, the letters between Knox and Anne Lock indicate a rather more mutual giving and receiving of friendship and assistance. A glance at aspects of their correspondence shines an important light on another side of Knox, as pastor and friend to two very different women.

The close relationship between Knox and Elizabeth Bowes lasted most of the rest of her life after Knox burst onto the scene in Berwick in 1549. She heard him preach, and from then on she sought his spiritual advice as she converted to Protestantism and tried to work out what it meant to live with integrity in her new faith. The many, many letters that Elizabeth Bowes wrote to Knox mainly concern her struggles to find assurance in her faith. How could she know that she was saved, that she was of God's elect? She was unsure whether there were enough fruits of faith in her life to be clear about her eternal standing. Were the trials and troubles that she faced a sign of God's displeasure against her? Knox deals with her seemingly endless and extremely repetitive doubts, questions, and anxieties with much compassion and patience (and just occasionally, some very understandable flashes of exasperation!). He tried to help her to see that she could be extremely overscrupulous and self-absorbed, and he sought to point her away from herself to Christ and to entrust in what he had done for her, rather than focusing on her doubts about whether she was doing enough for him. As he suggested to her, complacency and indifference on spiritual matters were far more likely to be signs of dubious standing before God than an earnest desire to be right with him, and she was in no danger of either of those two spiritual problems! Whether as a pastoral strategy or because it was true, or both, Knox also sometimes shared with Mrs. Bowes that her spiritual struggles were a mirror for his own and that giving her assistance was a help to him as well.

In addition to his letters, Knox took the time to write a treatise for her on Psalm 6, in an attempt to give her comfort in her spiritual difficulties. This brief psalm sees David deeply troubled and struggling under the apparent displeasure of God, until at the close he receives again the assurance of God's loving kindness. Knox uses this text to help Mrs. Bowes to realize that even the elect of God experience his chastising and his apparent absence. Knox urges her to follow David's example and continue to turn to God as her hope and help even when she does not feel his presence, because he will indeed show himself merciful to all who turn humbly to him. She must trust in God's goodness even in her felt darkness.

Here, then, in his pastoral concern for Elizabeth Bowes, we see a very different side to Knox's writing, as well as to his public persona. Knox doesn't just write controversial

tracts and treatises and letters, he also writes generous and gracious letters of spiritual encouragement; and he doesn't just write a lengthy (and somewhat tedious!) treatise on predestination, here we see him helping someone to wrestle with the personal implications of the doctrine.

With regard to Mrs. Lock, the surviving letters are from 1556–62, and they indicate a more rounded relationship between her and Knox than that between Knox and Elizabeth Bowes. Knox was close friends with both Anne and her first husband, Henry, and often stayed with them when he was in London. Anne was a highly educated (and as we will see in a moment, a highly talented) woman from a prominent family. Her father, Stephen Vaughan, was an international financier and diplomat. Her husband was a wealthy Protestant fabrics merchant. You might remember that she was one of many Protestant women who went into exile during Mary Tudor's reign, while their husbands remained in England. It was Knox himself who strongly encouraged her to come to the haven of Geneva. He made very clear in his letters to her that he felt it would be much safer for her in Geneva and also that he would greatly delight in her presence there. As he put it in a letter from November 1556, "If I should express the thirst . . . which I have had for your presence, I should appear to pass measure."[2] You might also remember one of Knox's most famous quotes, about Geneva being "the most perfect school of Christ since the days of the apostles." There is no doubt about his high opinion of life in Geneva, but there is also no doubt that he was wanting to paint the most persuasively attractive picture possible of life there. This quote is from a letter to Anne Lock in which he is pulling out all the stops to try to convince her to come. He was successful.

The letter was written in December of 1556, and she and her two children duly arrived in 1557, although one of her children died shortly after. To while away her time in exile, she translated some of Calvin's sermons on Isaiah, and she may well have written the first published sonnet sequence in English. She appended her *A Meditation of a Penitent*

Sinner, a series of sonnets based on Psalm 51, to her translation of Calvin's sermons.[3]

As all this might suggest, in her friendship with Knox,
Anne Lock was able to be the kind of spiritual and intellectual partner for him that Mrs. Bowes could never be, and
their correspondence reflects this. While Knox did indeed
provide Mrs. Lock and some other women in her circle with
spiritual counsel when requested, their relationship is not
rooted in the kind of spiritual neediness that characterizes
the letters from Mrs. Bowes to which Knox responded, and
Knox also turns to the ever-resourceful Mrs. Lock for various kinds of assistance. He would often call on her to convey
messages or request information on the latest developments
in England, and sometimes to seek her help in raising financial aid from leading English Protestants for the cause of the
Reformation in Scotland. Many of those who had been part
of the English congregation of exiles in Geneva remained in
close contact when it was safe for them to return to England, and Knox continues to refer to them as the "little
flock" in his correspondence with Anne, who is frequently
Knox's go-between for giving and receiving news of them.

He also asked her to send him books, including the
request in 1559 for her to send him the latest edition of
Calvin's *Institutes,* then hot off the presses, and that would
prove to be the final Latin edition. He later sent her a copy
of *The Scots Confession.* He was also extremely frank with her
in his assessment of the religious settlement in England
under Elizabeth I, criticizing the remaining "dregs of
papistry" in the English church and calling it a "bastard
religion." The context for his bluntness was Mrs. Lock's
uncertainty over whether to withdraw from the Church of
England. She sought his counsel on this over several letters
in 1559, and in his replies, Knox indicated his contempt for
The Book of Common Prayer and the insufficiently reformed

church, stating, among other things, that "We ought not to justifie with our presence such a mingle mangle as is now commaunded in your kirks." Later in the same letter, he seems to imply that Mrs. Lock has in fact already stopped attending her parish church. Patrick Collinson takes this as suggesting that perhaps Mrs. Lock is the first documented Elizabethan separatist.[4]

As well, Knox shared with Anne the latest progress with regard to the Reformation in Scotland. Indeed, Collinson calls these letters "almost . . . an early draft of the *History*" because of the detail that Knox includes in what he writes to her.[5] More so than in *The History of the Reformation in Scotland*, though, in these letters we see glimpses of Knox the private person rather than Knox the public prophet, as he expresses his personal hopes and disappointments. He admits to feeling afraid at times, and he expresses his frustration that the Reformation in Scotland seems to be more about destruction than rebuilding. It was all very well to

smash down statues and tear up vestments, for example, but where was the zeal for a renewed ministry? And when Mary, Queen of Scots, came to take up the throne, Knox expressed his bitter disappointment at the compliant attitude of many of the nobility and the infighting between them that jeopardized the prospects of a strong Protestant settlement.

What shines out of Knox's letters to Mrs. Lock is the depth of his care and respect and trust, and also her role as a confidante and help to him. No one reading these letters (or, indeed, those to Mrs. Bowes) could ever think of Knox as a despiser of women, chronically incapable of dealing with them as fellow human beings. From all the evidence, it seems that Knox was perfectly capable of showing great warmth, pastoral sensitivity, and personal integrity when dealing with intense and potentially complex relationships with women who valued him as much as he them. Given the mythical portrait of Knox as a hater of women that has been passed down in history and folklore, this corrective is a good place to end our portrait of his life and times and turn to a few reflections on his legacy.

CONCLUSION

Knox was a difficult and divisive figure in his own time, and he still is. He isn't easy to come to grips with, either in terms of his life, the role he played in history, or his writing, but we should at least try to come to grips with as many different aspects of him as possible. We've seen something of the range of his character, his writing, and his role: from fiery prophet to caring friend, from someone who advocates regicide to someone who provides pastoral comfort, from a central player in the crisis of a nation to an awkward presence on the periphery. One of the aims of this book has been to try to paint a portrait of Knox that is more than the caricature sketch that leads many of us to think we know all there is to know about him in a sentence or two.

A fuller sense of Knox in relation to his own time and context is one thing, but how have Knox and his legacy lived on into ours?

On the one hand, look in the right places and you can catch glimpses of Knox, his time, and his legacy everywhere. So, for example, in Edinburgh, take the steep climb up The Mound from Princes Street and enter the courtyard of New College. There you will be confronted by a massive statue of Knox, one arm clutching a Bible, the other outstretched in exhortation. Continue up the last stretch of the hill and round the corner to the Royal Mile. If you turn right you'll head up to Edinburgh Castle, scene of so many of the events that shaped Knox's life and Scotland's history during this period. Heading down the Royal Mile you can visit St. Giles, where he was a minister and from where he thundered against Mary, Queen of Scots, in her Palace of Holyrood at the bottom of the Mile. There is another statue of him in St. Giles, incidentally—though Knox himself would surely have been outraged at the idea of any statues of himself at all, especially one within a place of worship! A little farther down the Mile you can even visit the "John Knox House," filled with relics from his life and times (although it is by no means certain that he ever lived there). Go to St Andrews and you can see the places where Patrick Hamilton and Knox's hero, George Wishart, were burned at the stake. You can walk through the grounds of St. Mary's College, the University's Divinity School. You can explore the ruined Castle, with its many signs of the siege that led Knox to his imprisonment in the French galleys. You can worship at Holy Trinity parish church, where Knox preached his first sermon, where he returned in triumph in 1559, and where, toward the close of his life, the fire in his belly despite his physical frailty still held fifteen-year-old James Melville spellbound. You can wander the ruined Cathedral that was ransacked after Knox's fiery sermons in 1559 and that fell into disuse in the aftermath of the Reformation. There are many places where the stones still speak of Knox and the people and events that swirled around him.

On the other hand, you could also look to the living stones (1 Pet. 2:5). Millions of Christians the world over have come to faith and grown in discipleship through Presbyterian churches that owe their existence to the particular way that the Scottish Reformation took shape. The Church of Scotland did not develop its fully fledged Presbyterian order until after Knox's death, but Knox is at the heart of the Reformed Protestant settlement that forms the basis of all these daughter churches. In a double irony, it is also to a great extent through the influence of the Church of Scotland that the Westminster Confession and Catechisms have spread throughout the world. This is because it was Scotland (and not England where they were written) that took the Westminster standards to its heart and, from there, took them around the world. The double irony, of course, is that in adopting the Westminster standards in 1647, *The Scots Confession*, which Knox had a hand in writing, fell into relative neglect. Even so, it still holds its place among the Reformed confessions, and today is most readily accessible to many in the *Book of Confessions* published by the Presbyterian Church (U.S.A.) as part of its Constitution.

There is tangible evidence of the history that shaped Knox and that he helped to make. There is the living legacy of Christians throughout the world shaped by the church that Knox helped to found. But what about Knox's works and his ideas? Well, one of the things that getting to know Knox can teach us is that in some very important ways, we have to let him stay in his own time. With Knox, more than with many other theologians of his era, his writing is so intensively bound up with specific historical events that we can't simply transplant his ideas into our time and place. And for that matter, it also means that neither should we sit too easily in judgment on what he said and did. We have to respect him first and foremost as a man of his time.

What, though, might twenty-first-century Christians learn from Knox? Even if we do not follow him in his precise words or actions, perhaps we can be prompted to attempt to wrestle afresh with the same kinds of questions that he sought to answer. For example, what does it mean for current Christians to be faithful to Christ in the face of cultural pressure to march to the beat of a different drum (which is the strongest description those of us in democratic societies open to the Christian faith can use) or systematic and violent persecution (which is the reality for so many brothers and sisters in other contexts)? How do we discern

the presence, activity, and will of God in our time and place as we reflect on the patterns of God's dealings with his people in Scripture? And, taking up one of the main the priorities in Knox's life and work, what are the idolatries around us? Who or what is it that seeks our worship in place of God or seeks to distort our worship of God? And if we do not accept Knox's answers to those kinds of questions, perhaps we could at least find some inspiration—and challenge—from his lifelong, wholehearted, passionate courage and commitment in the service of God as he understood it.

Notes

(Re) Introducing John Knox

1. Quoted in Henry R. Sefton, *John Knox: An Account of the Development of His Spirituality* (Edinburgh: St Andrew Press, 1993). Sefton has given modernized spelling to the original text, found in the six-volume *The Works of John Knox*, ed. David Laing (Edinburgh: Woodrow Society, 1846–1864), 6:229. Hereafter this will be referred to as *Works*.

1: From Roman Catholic Priest to Protestant Galley Slave

1. At one stage it was thought that Knox was born in 1505, but this was based on an error in a seventeenth-century biography. Information about his life comes from Knox's own writings—in particular *The History of the Reformation in Scotland* and surviving letters—in addition to the writings of contemporaries about him. The standard biographies are Jasper Ridley, *John Knox* (Oxford: Oxford University Press, 1968) and W. Stanford Reid, *Trumpeter of God: A Biography of John Knox* (New York: Charles Scribner's Sons, 1974). For a more contemporary and highly readable account of his life, see Rosalind K. Marshall, *John Knox* (Edinburgh: Birlinn, 2000).

2. The standard edition of his writings is *Works*; there is also a two-volume, modernized edition of *The History of the Reformation in Scotland*, edited by William Croft Dickinson (Edinburgh: Nelson, 1949), hereafter, Dickinson. Page numbers for *The History of the Reformation in Scotland* will refer to the Dickinson edition.

Notes

3. For an excellent brief overview of the Reformation in this series, see Glenn S. Sunshine, *The Reformation for Armchair Theologians* (Louisville, KY: Westminster John Knox Press, 2005). For an outstanding lengthier account, see Diarmaid MacCulloch, *Reformation: Europe's House Divided, 1490–1700* (London: Penguin, 2004). The U.S. title is *The Reformation: A History.* For a more theologically focused introduction to the period, see Alister E. McGrath, *Reformation Thought: An Introduction*, 4th ed. (Oxford: Blackwell, 2012).
4. Dickinson, 1:81–86.
5. Ibid.,108–9.
6. Ibid., 97, 107–8.
7 From Martin Luther's *The Freedom of a Christian*, in John Dillenberger, ed., *Martin Luther: Selections from his Writings* (New York: Anchor, 1962), 60.
8. Richard G. Kyle and Dale W. Johnson, *John Knox: An Introduction to His Life and Works* (Eugene, OR: Wipf & Stock, 2009), 45.

2: From England to Exile

1. His response to the Council was later published as *A Vindication of the Doctrine That the Sacrifice of the Mass Is Idolatry, Works*, 3:33–70. This will be the subject of key text 2.
2. The letter can be found in Peter Lorimer, *John Knox and the Church of England: His Work in Her Pulpit and His Influence upon Her Liturgy, Articles, and Parties* (London: Henry S. King & Co., 1875), 260–61.
3. Dickinson, 1:118.
4. *Works*, 3:376–78.
5. Council of Trent Session XXII, the Doctrine on the Sacrifice of the Mass.
6. For Roman Catholics, the irredeemably wicked would go to hell, the saints would go straight to heaven, and most people would end up in purgatory for a period of time before reaching heaven. Protestants rejected belief in purgatory as unscriptural.

7. *Works,* 3:157–216.
8. *Works,* 3:251–330.

3: A Turbulent Exile

1. See Richard L. Greaves, *Theology & Revolution in the Scottish Reformation: Studies in the Thought of John Knox* (Washington DC: Christian University Press, 1980), 132–33. This is somewhat similar to the position that Calvin eventually came to express in the 1559 edition of the *Institutes,* where his view is that while subjects in general may not rebel, members of the ruling class may instigate the removal of an ungodly tyrant, but only as a very last resort after all other means of persuasion have proved to be futile. There is still a good deal more ambivalence and reluctance in Calvin's position than Viret's, however.
2. *Works,* vol. 4:59.
3. Roger A. Mason, ed., *Knox: On Rebellion* (Cambridge: Cambridge University Press, 1994), xiv.
4. The Geneva Bible was also the version of choice for those seeking the fullest reformation of the church in England from its first publication until the 1630s. These Puritans held strongly to the Geneva Bible and emphatically refused to use the Authorized or King James version of 1611, which James I commissioned in part to combat the influence of the Geneva Bible—the marginal notes of which he loathed. The Geneva Bible declined in use from the 1630s because Charles I's Archbishop of Canterbury, William Laud, banned domestic printing of it, and then its importation from abroad, in an attempt to enforce the use of the King James version instead. The Geneva Bible was one of the most important versions taken to America by the pilgrims, who were themselves escaping from the persecutions of Charles I and Archbishop Laud.
5. From a letter to Anne Lock, December 9, 1556, *Works,* 4:240.
6. Dickinson, 1:137.
7. For convenient access to the text of the *First Blast* see Mason, *Knox: On Rebellion.* Mason brings together the *First Blast*

and major texts in relation to the situation in Scotland along with extracts from Knox's *The History of the Reformation in Scotland*. A minimum of alterations, mainly to the spelling, makes this an excellent place to start for an accessible version of some of Knox's most important works.

8. Roger A. Mason, "Knox, Resistance and the Royal Supremacy" in Mason, ed., *John Knox and the British Reformations* (Aldershot: Ashgate, 1998), 170–71.

9. Mason, *Knox: On Rebellion*, 98. In fact, when it came to it, Knox did not call for the execution of Mary of Guise, only her deposition. Mason observes (p. xx) that this is almost certainly because Scotland had not formally accepted Protestantism, and so had not yet become a "covenanted" nation. Later he made strident calls for the execution of Mary, Queen of Scots, because by that time Scotland had indeed adopted Protestantism and so Queen Mary was guilty of trying to break the covenant that the nation had made with God.

10. Ibid., 85.

11. Ibid., 102.

12. Ibid., 103.

13. Kyle and Johnson, *John Knox,* 105–6.

14. Mason, *Knox: On Rebellion*, 124.

4: Returning to a Revolution

1. *Works*, 6:14.

2. Dickinson, 1:282–87.

3. Dickinson, 1:351.

4. In addition to affirming his general closeness to Calvin (*Works*, 1:31), Knox quotes from Calvin's *Institutes*, from his treatise *Concerning the Eternal Predestination of God*, and from his commentary on Isaiah, and refers to Theodore Beza's tract against Sebastian Castellio on the subject. Knox refers to Beza's twenty-nine propositions on election in this tract as "the sum of our doctrine on this matter" (ibid., 189).

5. All citations in this paragraph are from *The Scots Confession*, chapter 21, which can be found in the *Book of Confessions*

(Louisville, KY: Office of the General Assembly, Presbyterian Church (U.S.A.), 1999), 21-22. The *Book of Confessions* can also be downloaded as a PDF at http://www.pcusa.org/resource/book-confessions/.

5: A Roman Catholic Queen and a Protestant Realm

1. Cited in Ridley, *John Knox*, 390.
2. Dickinson, 2:13–20.
3. For the accounts of the second and third (two-part) meetings, see ibid., 43–46, 71–74.
4. Ibid., 82–84.
5. Ibid., 92–93.
6. For an account of the proceedings, see Ridley, *John Knox*, 435–37.
7. *Works*, 6:lxvii.
8. R. Pitcairn, ed., *The Autobiography and Diary of Mr. James Melvill* (Edinburgh: Woodrow Society, 1842), 33.
9. For the tract and also the letter included as an appendix, see *Works*, 6:479–520, 617–18.

6: More than Marys

1. For summaries of Knox's relationship with women in general and Mrs. Bowes and Mrs. Lock in particular, see Patrick Collinson, "John Knox, the Church of England and the Women of England," in Mason, ed., *John Knox and the British Reformations*, 74–96; and Susan M. Felch, "Deir Sister": The Letters of John Knox to Anne Vaughan Lok," *Renaissance and Reformation* 19.4 (1995): 47–68 and her "The Rhetoric of Biblical Authority: John Knox and the Question of Women," *The Sixteenth-Century Journal* 26 (1995): 805–22.
2. *Works*, 4:237.
3. Henry Lock clearly approved of and delighted in his wife's talents, writing an admiring inscription in his copy of the book. Their son Henry became a minor religious poet. After the death of her first husband in 1571, Anne married the Puritan preacher Edward Dering in 1572, and then after his

death in 1576, Richard Prowse, who was the mayor of Exeter.

4. See Collinson, "John Knox, the Church of England and the Women of England," in Mason, ed, *John Knox and the British Reformations*, 91–92.

5. Ibid, 84–85.

For Further Reading

Knox's writings

The standard edition of Knox's works is Laing, David, ed., *The Works of John Knox*. 6 vols. (Edinburgh: Woodrow Society, 1846–64).

There is also a modernized edition of *The History of the Reformation in Scotland*, ed. William Croft Dickinson (Edinburgh: Nelson, 1949).

For a modernized selection of texts and extracts related to Knox's theological reflections on political issues and a helpful introductory essay: Mason, Roger A., ed., *Knox: On Rebellion* (Cambridge: Cambridge University Press, 1994).

You can find the text of *The Scots Confession* in *Book of Confessions* (Louisville, KY: Office of the General Assembly, Presbyterian Church (U.S.A.), 1999), also accessible as a downloadable pdf from their Web site: http://www.pcusa.org/resource/book-confessions/.

Short extracts from a wider range of Knox's work can be found in Sefton, Henry R., *John Knox: An Account of the Development of His Spirituality* (Edinburgh: St. Andrew Press, 1998). This slim volume also contains an overview of his life.

About Knox

There are two standard biographies: Ridley, Jasper, *John Knox* (Oxford: Oxford University Press, 1968). Stanford Reid, W., *Trumpeter of God: A Biography of John Knox* (New York: Scribner, 1974).

For Further Reading

There is also a more contemporary and less formal account of his life: Marshall, Rosalind K., *John Knox* (Edinburgh: Birlinn, 2000).

For an overview of his life and outlines of his major writings, see Kyle, Richard G. and Dale W. Johnson, *John Knox: An Introduction to His Life and Works* (Eugene, OR: Wipf & Stock, 2009).

For essays on several aspects of his life and work, see Mason, Roger A. *John Knox and the British Reformations* (Aldershot: Ashgate, 1998).

Index

153

Index

Index

CPSIA information can be obtained at www.ICGtesting.com
Printed in the USA
LVOW10s0103170614

390289LV00011B/121/P

9 780664 236694